AN ENCOURAGING WORD

AN ENCOURAGING WORD

Renewed Hearts, Renewed Church

J. RONALD KNOTT

Foreword by Michael Downey

CROSSROAD · NEW YORK

1997

The Crossroad Publishing Company
370 Lexington Avenue, New York, NY 10017

Printed in the United States of America

Library of Congress Cataloging-in-Publication Data
Knott, J. Ronald.
    An encouraging word: renewed hearts, renewed church / J. Ronald
Knott ; foreword by Michael Downey.
        p. cm.
    ISBN 0-8245-1479-3 (pbk.)
    1. Catholic Church—Sermons.   2. Sermons, American.   I. Title.
BX1756.K67E53   1995
252'.02—dc20   94-49556
                                                                    CIP

To my good friend
Jeanne Paradis,
who consistently encouraged me
to share these words
with a broader audience

For the vision still has its time,
presses on to fulfillment,
and will not disappoint;

If it delays, wait for it,
it will surely come,
it will not be late.

— HABAKKUK 2:3

Contents

— ✠ —

9

LOVE STORIES

Acknowledgments

My deepest gratitude goes to Archbishop Thomas C. Kelly, O.P., who entrusted the pulpit of the Cathedral of the Assumption to me in 1983 and who has encouraged me every step of the way in its renewal.

To the parish council of the cathedral; to the board, staff, and committee members of the Cathedral Heritage Foundation, particularly Christy Brown and Trish Pugh Jones, with whom I have shared leadership; and especially to the cathedral staff: Julie Wise Zoeller, Elaine M. Winebrenner, David B. Lang, Patricia A. Sexton, Mary Kay Tubello, Deacon Pat Wright, Jerre Bassett, Stanley Barr, Mary Ballard, Charlotte Hazas, Lanese Cox, and Larry Love, I also express my deepest gratitude. These are the people who have done the daily hard work to implement the vision of a renewed cathedral. My heartfelt thanks go as well to the priests with whom I have shared the privilege of preaching at the cathedral on a regular basis: Joe Vest, Peyton Badgett, Bill Medley, Joe Stoltz, and Marty Linebach.

I thank the monks of St. Meinrad Archabbey in Indiana, who first modeled for me the transforming power of good preaching. And I am grateful to the people who have listened to me preach over the years, consistently offering their affirmation, encouragement, and suggestions, especially the parishioners of St. John Vianney, St. Mildred, St. Peter, Good Shepherd, Holy Name of Mary, and the Cathedral of the Assumption.

I am thankful for my deceased parents, Jim and Ethel, and deeply grateful to my brothers and sisters, Brenda, Gary, Lois, Nancy, Kaye, and Mark, who have flooded me with support and encouragement during my years as a priest. I thank my surrogate parents here in Louisville, Paul and Wilhemine King, who would do just about anything to help me.

I am indebted to John Long, who first raised the real possibility of publishing a collection of homilies. I am also most grateful to Dr. Michael Downey, who carefully and thoughtfully saw this volume through publication. Thanks also to Lynn Schmitt, my editor at the Crossroad Publishing Company.

Finally, a very special thank you goes to my friend Becky Hollingsworth, who types and edits my homily every week, does research for me, and who typed and retyped the manuscript for this book. I could not have done this without her generous assistance.

Foreword

One of the most enduring legacies of the Second Vatican Council is its affirmation of the centrality of Scripture in the liturgy and in Christian living. In the decades since the council there has been a flourishing of Bible study groups, parish renewal programs, prayer meetings, participation in retreats of all sorts, and an ever-widening interest in spiritual growth and maturation on the part of all the baptized. Many of these developments are directly related to the council's emphasis on the singular importance of the word and its formative role in Christian prayer, worship, and the life of discipleship. Perhaps more than anything else, Christian spirituality since the council has been a biblical and liturgical spirituality.

It should come as no surprise, then, that increasing numbers of Roman Catholics express a strong desire for good preaching of the word. They know that what is said and done in the liturgy is to be brought to bear on their everyday lives. And they expect that what is proclaimed and heard from the pulpit will challenge them and encourage them in this task. Even though there is always a gap between what is expected and what actually takes place, it is quite startling to find so many Catholics who are disheartened and disappointed by what is said from the parish pulpit.

In 1983, Ronald Knott was asked by his bishop to leave his parish in rural Kentucky to become pastor of the Roman Catholic Cathedral of the Assumption in Louisville. In the heart of the city, the cathedral was not unlike many other inner city churches: few parishioners on the rolls, low attendance at Sunday Mass and other liturgical services, diminishing financial resources, and a growing number of urban poor flocking to the door for material rather than spiritual sustenance. When Father Knott asked what was expected of him in his new assignment, Archbishop Thomas Kelly replied: "Just do something with it!"

Today the Cathedral of the Assumption is a vibrant and thriving community of faith and worship. People come from miles around to celebrate Sunday Eucharist at Louisville's cathedral. And folks from the inner city, previously unseen and unheard in that dilapidated old church, now lift their voices in praise and thanks to God in this assembly.

A church in shambles has been renewed. The building has been renovated. There has been an expansion of liturgical services. Hospitality has been extended to a wide range of persons and groups. The cathedral has become a center of ecumenical and interreligious dialogue. Those active in the cathedral's social outreach programs continually redouble efforts to meet the needs of a great diversity of people who are marginal to both society and church. This once sagging, grimy, red brick structure has become what every cathedral was meant to be from early Christian centuries to the present: the heart of the local church.

The renewal of the cathedral has involved far more than the renovation of a church building. The hearts of those who gather for worship have been renewed through ongoing participation in word and sacrament. Day by day, week by week, those who celebrate Christ's mysteries in word and sacrament have become what they celebrate: the Body of Christ, the church. Central to the task of being and building the Body of Christ is the proclamation and hearing of the word in the assembly of faith and worship. The word in worship invites all who hear it to ever fuller participation in communion with God in Christ through the Spirit. It is a word that enlightens, instructs, enlivens, guides, and heals. It is an encouraging word.

In any experience of new life, there is a profound awareness of what a gift it is. This is no less true of the flourishing of Christian life at Louisville's cathedral. But this renewal has been due in no small way to Ron Knott's efforts to take the bishop's mandate with utmost seriousness: "Just do something with it." What Father Knott has done is to make every effort to preach the word of God and preach it well. When asked why they come from "out of the woodwork," parishioners from near and far state forthrightly: good preaching.

Ronald Knott's homilies have been gathered together so that they might give an encouraging word to all who look to Christ as a source of healing and hope. They have been arranged in view of the unfolding of the Christian mystery: from anticipation of Christ's coming, through his life, ministry, and death, to his resurrection and new life in the church through the presence and power of the Holy Spirit. Offered now to those in the wider church who recognize the need to be washed in the word, to be attentive to the rhythms of the word throughout the year, these words will be all the more profitable when read together with those passages from Scripture which they seek to illuminate. Because it is the Word itself, a Word beneath and beyond all words, for which the human heart longs and in which it finds its rest. This Word beneath and beyond all telling is a Word whose name is mercy revealed in the suffering love of the cross. If there be encouragement in the Word it is this: The power of suffering love prevails over all evil. God's mercy endures forever! And in the ways and works and words of mercy we can discern God's signature in the church and in the world.

MICHAEL DOWNEY

AN ANCIENT LOVE

Repent! The Kingdom Is at Hand!

Make ready the way of the Lord,
  Clear him a straight path.
Every valley shall be filled
  And every mountain and hill shall be leveled.
The windings shall be made straight,
  And the rough ways smooth.

— LUKE 3:4–5

MY MOTHER was a pretty calm person, at least externally. But once in a while she would "freak out" in a panic attack. One thing would always launch her into orbit: when she saw the parish priest drive by the house. He was the kind who liked to drop in on people. If he ever passed the house and she noticed the car, she went to pieces. It was like hearing a newsbreak that the Russians had pushed the button and the bomb was on the way. Our pastor in those days was the kind who would sit in a chair in his shiny shoes and French cuffs and pick lint off his black coat as he talked to you. With a house full of kids, seven of us in all, the place usually looked like a bomb had already gone off. Our lint was as big as snowballs.

As a result of all this, my mother trained us like a little civil defense corps. In a matter of minutes, we could clear a path, fill in the deep holes, and make the rough ways smooth so that Father could drop in and visit. Usually he didn't stop, but we were trained for active duty at a moment's notice. To this day, I try never to drop in on people, because I have this awful feeling that people inside the house are sweating blood just seeing a black suit coming toward the door.

In the part of the world in which our Sacred Scriptures were written, when a king proposed to visit a part of the kingdom, he never just "dropped in." He usually sent ambassadors ahead in plenty of time to tell the people to prepare the roads. It was hard enough in those days to travel, but the road system was primitive in most places — often just paths or animal traces. When people heard the king was coming, they set to fixing the roads to make his trip smooth. Sharp curves had to be straightened; rock slides had to be cleared; rough terrain had to be leveled. This work made it easy for the king and his entourage to reach their destination.

John the Baptizer used this image in his preaching when he was trying to prepare people for the coming of Jesus, the Messiah. He wasn't speaking literally about road construction or house cleaning. He was talking about a change of heart, a change of attitude, a new way of thinking about things and looking at things. The rough edges, the crooked turns, and the blockages were in people's minds and hearts. Without this change of heart, people would not be able to see and understand and comprehend what was about to take place. They would simply miss it. They would not be open to receive it.

John called it "repentance." He preached repentance, or change of heart. He pleaded for a whole new outlook, a new set of values to live by, new ways of thinking about people and things, a fresh way of doing things. As the story unfolds, we realize that those who did not "repent," did not change their way of looking at things, did, indeed, miss Jesus Christ. They were looking in the wrong direction. Important things were not important to them. They were so frozen in their old way of thinking and seeing that they saw nothing. They were so convinced that they already knew how God was going to do things that they missed what God was actually doing. For instance, they thought the Messiah was going to be a majestic king who would cater to the rich and powerful. What God actually did was to be born in a barn and cater to the poor and forgotten.

Because they did not let go of their old way of seeing things and their old priorities, they missed what God was actually doing right under their noses. Because they did not repent, did not give up their old way of thinking, they saw in Jesus nothing more than a poor carpenter from Nazareth — a troublemaker for the government and a radical teacher who wanted to change that "old-time religion" of Abraham, Isaac, and Jacob. They did not change their minds or hearts or outlooks and therefore saw nothing and felt nothing in the person of Jesus. They missed the boat.

Each Christmas, a lot of people miss the boat because they try to celebrate Christmas without observing Advent. They look again in all the wrong places for that elusive "good feeling" that everybody would like to have. That good feeling cannot be accomplished by compulsive shopping and self-indulgence. That good feeling cannot be created by arranging externals. Each year people spend these five weeks in a frantic effort to create the "Christmas spirit." Each year we undergo that hollow feeling that somehow we missed it again. Each year, depression and suicide keep counselors' offices and funeral homes busy. Spending more, decorating more, and eating more will not make us feel good at Christmas.

The first step to having that elusive good feeling at Christmas is to "repent" of our traditional approach to celebrating this holiday by buying useless presents for people we don't like with money we don't have. A lot of our practice during the Christmas rush is a crime against the Christian faith. If we have the courage to step back and look at most of what we do at this time of year, we will have to own up to the fact that it has little or nothing to do with the birth of Jesus Christ. Jesus would have been outraged by most of it. It looks more like a pagan orgy of greed, self-indulgence, and waste than a remembrance of a stable-born friend of the poor and outcast.

The second step, after freeing ourselves from the whirlwind of a commercialized Christmas, is to focus on just why Jesus Christ was born to begin with. I am convinced that very few people, even lifelong Catholics, know why. Advent is a time to ponder that question.

Why in the world would God, Creator of the universe and everything in it, choose to become a human being, coming in the form of a little baby born to a dirt-poor family? After a life of perfect good, why would God choose to let those same people he came to save nail him to a cross between two common thieves? John the Baptist gives us the answer: He came to announce the kingdom. He said it has begun. It is small and quiet; it will grow gradually, doing battle with darkness in all its forms, until it has squeezed out all evil and replaced evil with life and goodness.

To understand it, you have to go back to the first pages of the Bible. There we read that in the beginning everything was good. We, beginning with our first parents, have chosen over and over to work against God. God promised that someday he would turn it all back to good again. That someday began with the birth of Jesus Christ.

Believe it or not, the world is being remade by God right now. Evil may win a lot more battles, but it will lose the war. No matter how powerful evil might appear to be, it will be defeated. The kingdom, a time when God's will for unity and harmony and wholeness and light and justice will be realized, *has already begun*. It is struggling for life. It has lots of enemies, but the good news is this: The kingdom will keep growing until we are back in the Garden of Eden. Call it heaven; call it the Parousia; call it glory; call it the Second Coming; call it what you might — it is coming and there is no power on earth that can stop it, not even the power of hell.

Knowing that and reflecting on that is what feeling good is all about. That is what peace is all about. The victory has been won. Good will win. Justice will come. So stop the hand wringing. Stop the worrying. It's happening all around you. Step by step, inch by inch, cell by cell, God's kingdom is coming. Only those who have been converted to see as God sees will see it. So, no matter what you're facing, no matter what your physical or financial condition, you can feel good just knowing that.

God has invited us to help him bring that kingdom to its fullness. He invites us, but also reminds us that whether or not we help, it will come. He invites us to change our way of seeing, our value system, our priorities. He told us that kingdom builders have certain godlike qualities, which Jesus outlined in the Beatitudes.

Once we are converted to seeing things as God sees them, becoming partners with him in building that kingdom, we will begin to understand that things will not make us or the world happy. Reverencing God and each other will do so. If our God has taught us that things will not make us happy, then why for God's sake has hysterical and wasteful spending become the major activity for celebrating the birth of a Savior who rejected it?

Once we are converted to seeing things as God sees them, becoming partners with him in building that kingdom, we will begin to understand that giving will make us happy — giving to the poor and suffering, not to the person who has everything. If our God chose to become poor, walk with the poor, identify himself with the poor, then why in God's name do we celebrate his birth by heaping more on those who already have too much?

Once we are converted to seeing things as God sees them, becoming partners with him in building that kingdom, we will begin to understand that hungering and thirsting for holiness will make us happy. If our Savior taught us that, then why for God's sake do we try to "get ready" for Christmas with a trivial, two-minute, quickie confession on Christmas Eve?

Repent! The kingdom is at hand! Advent gets snowed under every year. John the Baptist invites us to get ready for Christmas. He invites us to change the way we do things, the way we view things, the way we prioritize things. He invites us to see with God's eyes so that we can see God re-creating the world. God invites us to become partners with him in that re-creating and to celebrate its beginning in Jesus Christ. He invites us to cooperate with him until it comes to perfection. Maybe it is still not too late to get ready for Christmas.

Scripture Readings

BARUCH 5:1–9
PHILIPPIANS 1:3–6, 8–11
LUKE 3:1–6

The God Who Embraces Us

Elizabeth... cried out in a loud voice: "... But who am I that the mother of my Lord should come to me? The moment your greeting sounded in my ears, the baby leapt in my womb for joy."

— LUKE 1:41–44

IT AMAZES ME how many people I run into who really don't like God at all. I am not talking about atheists or agnostics. I mean churchgoing, believing people who have tried to relate to God all their lives. They fear God. They follow the rules. But they really don't like God much. He is feared, dreaded, and therefore remains out there on the edges of their lives somewhere. This dreaded God is kept at arm's length for all practical purposes. How tragic! God has bent over backward to show his love, but the message has not gotten through. I can understand this, because most of my life I haven't liked him much either. I believed in him. I feared him. But I never liked him all that much.

Many people experience God as a harsh, judgmental, and exacting despot. This mean God demands so much that it becomes impossible to measure up. Even a person's best does not seem good enough to please this God. This God, who is all-powerful, resembles a moody pagan god who has to be bribed to give any help at all. This God appears to love pain, suffering, and punishment, while withholding pleasure, success, and happiness until we're dead. Like the IRS, this God is avoided as much as possible. All people can do is hope that they make it through life without being caught and that there will be enough time to prepare for that big audit at the end of life.

After all God has done to prove his unconditional love for us, so many church people still haven't heard the good news. Why is that? I believe it is because we, as a church, have focused too much on what we are able to do for God rather than on what God has done for us. And because we have always done a spotty job of being perfect, we conclude that God's love is proportionate to how good we are. Many still believe that God's love and approval depends on earning it. It's a widely held belief: you're loved if you earn it. Since we are unable to be perfect, many conclude that God withholds love and acceptance in direct proportion to how good or bad we have been. But God has loved us, whether we deserve it or not. Many people still don't get it.

When you think about it, the evidence is there. When we were created, we were created in the image and likeness of God. Throughout history, God sent prophet after prophet to renew his vow to love us. He even compared his relationship to us to a marriage. He loved us through centuries of foolishness on our part. Even when we killed all his messengers, God sent his only Son as final proof of his love. This God in flesh was born in a barn. This Jesus, in story after story, told us that God loves the prodigal son as well as the perfect son, the lost sheep as well as the ninety-nine who stayed in line; and all get a full day's pay of his love, no matter how much or how little they worked.

Even when we killed God's Son, he still loved us. He left us bread and wine, his Body and Blood, as food for the journey. He promised to live inside us, making us walking tabernacles, until he comes to get us. He promised to take us, good and bad alike, to a heavenly banquet for all eternity. He said while we were still sinners: "I do not call you slaves but friends" (John 15:15). He even told us how we ought to feel about all this: deliriously happy as a person who has accidentally stumbled onto a buried treasure or the most exquisite pearl in the whole world.

But I don't see that response very often. How sad that a religion of love has been dwarfed into a religion of fear and legalism for too many people!

For most of my life I too feared God rather than loved God. But I had a marvelous religious experience that changed that. That experience is why I talk so much about God's unconditional love. My fear and dread of God and of judgment was lifted from my heart, literally overnight. It happened in a dream I had while I was in the missions in 1976. I dreamed God and I were sitting in those cheap, folding lawn chairs on top of a grass-carpeted, moundlike mountain. We were sitting side by side, watching the sunset. I couldn't look over, but I knew it was him. There was a pleasant, cool breeze blowing. We just sat there in silence, smoking King Edward cigars, side by side, watching a marvelous sunset. Finally, after quite a few minutes, God leaned over and said to me: "Ron, isn't this wonderful?" I woke up then. The dream was so clear and memorable that since the moment I woke up, I have never been afraid of God. We have had a friendship ever since. It was a shift, not of the mind, but of the heart. It was one of those moments of true grace.

I believe with all my heart that the God we celebrate at Christmas loves us all unconditionally; that he loves us in spite of our sins, failures, and stupidities. I have tried to convey that message to those of you who doubt God's love for you because of who you are or what you have done — the poor, the crazy, the divorced, the sexual minorities, those who have been away from the church, and those who feel unworthy and useless. When it's all said and done, that's what God wanted to tell us that first Christmas and every Christmas since.

Scripture Readings

MICAH 5:1–4
HEBREWS 10:5–10
LUKE 1:39–45

Emmanuel

*"And they shall name him Emmanuel," a name which means
"God is with us."*

— MATTHEW 1:23

C LYDE CREWS, a priest of the archdiocese of Louisville and
a professor of theology at Bellarmine College, has pub-
lished a book of old Catholic photographs collected over
a period of two hundred years. There are a lot of noteworthy
things about the book, but one thing is especially interesting.
There are a lot of photographs of nuns and schoolchildren, including a photograph taken in 1885 of two Sisters of Mercy and
a group of children from the cathedral school. What is interesting
about these photographs is how the children relate to the nuns.
They all seem to be trying to touch the sisters. Children have their
hands on the seated nuns' knees or their arms wrapped around
the sisters. Those who are unable to touch the sisters lean toward the nuns in full habit. There seems to be a genuine love and
tenderness between the sisters and their pupils. Missing is any evidence of those trite old stories of poor kids mistreated by mean
nuns. Rather, it appears from many of the photos that the kids
cannot help snuggling up to sister.

I am convinced that if the Bible had been a collection of photographs, there would be many pictures of God as someone trying
to snuggle up to his people. The Bible is filled with word pictures
and stories of God trying to get closer to us. In fact, if you read
it carefully and completely, you get the idea that God has tried
throughout history to gather us to himself. And we read story
after story about human beings pushing him away.

Matthew's gospel tells us that the newborn Christ Child is to be called Emmanuel, a word that means "God is with us." I think this is one of the most appropriate names for God. It describes what God has been up to better than any other name.

From the very beginning God has been trying to draw us near. Like those kids in the old cathedral school photographs, God has always tried to touch us. The stories are sprinkled everywhere through the sacred Book. Isaiah the prophet tells us that God is like a shepherd who feeds his flock and gathers the lambs in his arms, holding them carefully close to his heart, leading them home. Jesus looks out over the holy city of Jerusalem shortly before his death and says these words: "Oh, Jerusalem, Jerusalem!...How often have I yearned to gather your children, as a mother bird gathers her young under her wings, but you refused me" (Matthew 23:37). In the creation story, God not only creates a perfect garden for Adam and Eve, he walks in the garden with them.

One of the Scriptures' choicest images of our relationship with God is that of marriage. God is pictured as the patient husband who keeps taking back his wayward wife. He is so lovesick for his spouse and wants to be with her so much that he keeps taking her back, over and over again. Many of Jesus' parables bespeak God's desire to have us around him. The father throws his arms around his prodigal son and kisses him. The lost sheep is thrown over the good shepherd's shoulders and carried home in jubilation. The woman who found a single lost coin calls the neighbors in for a party. The vineyard owner gives everybody a full day's pay, no matter when they started working. God spoils his children rotten with love!

Before Jesus left this earth, he promised to come back and take us all to be with him in his Father's house, which has rooms enough for everybody. At the end of Matthew's gospel, Jesus promised to be with us always, even to the end of time. He sent the Holy Spirit to live within us so that we would not be orphaned. God has been with his people in so many ways. He has led them with pillars of fire, stars, and leaders like Moses. He has fed them with manna in the desert and water from the rock. He has delivered them from slavery and exile.

We certainly do have a God who is with us. We have a God who has always wanted to be at our side in this life. We have a God who wants us at his side in the next life. But nowhere do we see God trying to get close to us more than during Advent, the time of year when we celebrate God taking on human flesh. He loves us enough to go so far as to become one of us. What good news! What unbelievable love! The Creator of the universe and everything in it, walking side by side with us, suffering all we suffer, like us in all things but sin.

Every weekend when we gather in the Cathedral of the Assumption, be it Christmas or Easter, Lent or Pentecost, wedding or funeral, baptism or ordination, we celebrate Emmanuel, God with us. The night before he died, Jesus gave himself to us in the form of bread and wine. In this sacred meal, God gets inside us and we become what we eat. By feeding on his Body and Blood, we become the Body of Christ, empowered to carry on his work of love and compassion, healing, peacemaking, encouragement, and hope. Yes, God is truly with us.

The word *companion* comes from the Latin word for "eating bread with." A companion is one you share your bread with. We have a God who is our companion. He shares his bread with us. He walks with us, as he did on the road to Emmaus, even when we do not see him. We remember over and over again that our God is with us. He is a companion. He wants us with him. He is Emmanuel.

Scripture Readings

MICAH 5:1–4
HEBREWS 10:5–10
LUKE 1:39–45

LOVE COME DOWN

Maybe This Will Grab Their Attention

The Word became flesh and made his dwelling among us.
— JOHN 1:14

KNOW THAT it is self-incriminating to admit this and I probably don't need to give anyone any more ammunition, but I'm an avid reader of *Leo,* the Louisville Eccentric Organization's free bimonthly paper. I am especially fond of the column "News from the Weird." It is a collection of weird experiences from real life. One of my recent favorites is a story about a thirty-eight-year-old man who was hospitalized in Princeton, West Virginia, in October with gunshot wounds. He had been drinking and reported accidentally shooting himself three times as he attempted to clean each of his three guns. He said the first shot didn't hurt, the second "stung a little," and the third "really hurt," prompting him to call an ambulance.

Some people just don't get the point. You have to rub their noses in it. In a way, that is what Christmas is all about. "In times past, God spoke in fragmentary and varied ways to our [ancestors] through the prophets; in this, the final age, he has spoken to us through his Son" (Hebrews 1:1). Ever since the big mess-up in the Garden of Eden, God has never quit loving us, never quit reaching out to us, never let up on his gift-giving.

The Old Testament prophets put it into graphic bedroom language: We are pursued by a God in heat. He doesn't just love us in some polite way from a distance; he can't keep his hands off us. He pursues us like a hunting dog, no matter how frigid our response to him might be. He tried to get the point across using various people, signs, and wonders, but it wasn't getting through. So he took on human flesh, lived among us, and taught us about Abba, that doting parent of a God who was the center of all Jesus' stories. Even after we spat on God's gift and nailed it to a tree, he continued to love us.

That's what all this is about. We need not see the pregnant virgin, singing angels, poor shepherds, foreign astrologers, stinking stables, and a "baby God" as stumbling blocks. Remember, God is trying to get a message across. What is important is the message. What is important is that God is making a statement to us. We must really be loved for God to go to this much trouble. That's the point that's always missed. Christmas is not about God's love for Jesus but about God's love for us. This Christmas thing is the passionate act of a God who is eaten up with love for us.

Even after nearly two thousand Christmases, most people still just don't get it — the fact that we are deeply loved, and loved without condition. Churches still tend to "conditionalize" this message, robbing it of its power to transform people's lives. We see this in its ugliest form in the right-wing fundamentalism that has invaded so many churches recently, including ours. God's unconditional love, announced with clarity and conviction, is still powerfully attractive to people. But these Christo-Fascists replace God's power with their own coercive power. "By God, we'll force people to be good, if we have to!" For all their God-talk, they still miss the point, creating a God in their own image and likeness — a judgmental, nitpicking, and get-even God.

The point of our gathering at Christmas is this: The Creator of everything we see loves us deeply — almost insanely. Look underneath all this hoopla, and that is what you should see. If you can't see that, you have missed the point. You just don't get it.

What we celebrate at Christmas, the mystery of God's love for all human beings, makes the religious wars of India and Northern Ireland look absurd. When we celebrate God's love for all human beings, the race wars of South Africa and Los Angeles look sacrilegious. All that stuff comes from a belief that love is scarce, that there is not enough to go around, when in fact we are standing knee-deep in it right now.

Scripture Readings

ISAIAH 52:7–10
HEBREWS 1:1–6
JOHN 1:1–18

Medium vs. Message

"You have nothing to fear! I come to proclaim good news to you — tidings of great joy to be shared by the whole people. This day . . . a savior has been born to you, the Messiah and Lord."

— LUKE 2:10–11

I REMEMBER one clown in particular from childhood. He pulled a banana out of his pocket and peeled it, ever so ceremoniously. When he had peeled the last of the jacket from the banana, he threw away the banana and ate the peel. The crowd erupted with laughter. As I got older, I realized why that was so funny. It was not just a joke; it was an insight into human behavior. In many ways, we are always throwing out the banana and eating the peel. Whether it is people or food, packaging seems to be everything.

According to a recent article in *Newsweek* magazine, half of the American population claims a religion that does not inform their attitudes or behavior. Only 19 percent of adult Americans regularly practice their religion. We are a nation whose people claim to be religious but few take their faith seriously. We like the peel; we just don't care about the banana.

I heard a disc jockey recently talking about a couple who wanted a "church wedding" without the religion. They bought an old church for $2,500. We like the peel; we just don't care about the banana.

I saw a comedian recently who said he went into a grocery, walked up to the frozen food section, and picked up a lemon pie labeled "Made with artificial lemon flavoring." He wheeled by the furniture polish section, picked up a can, and read, "Made with real lemon juice." "What is wrong with this country?" he said. "We're eating the garbage and putting the good stuff on the furniture!" We like the peel; we just don't care about the banana.

Whether it's food, religion, "church weddings," or people — packaging seems to be everything. That's what made the clown so funny. He helped us see ourselves. In religion, there is an almost incurable human tendency to make the accidentals essential, and the essentials accidental; to make symbols *objects* of faith rather than the *means* of faith. Instead of the symbols being a means of communication between people and God, they become idols. The packaging becomes everything. We like the peel; we just don't care about the banana.

Nowhere is this more obvious than in our love for Christmas. It is so easy to get intoxicated on the cuteness of Christmas without ever getting beyond it. What we celebrate at Christmas is not cuteness but lightning. What we have here is not cuteness but a mind-blowing, history-making manifestation of God in human life: the Word become flesh.

God had something incredible to say and he used some very simple packaging to say it. Peel away the manger, star, shepherds, astrologers, and poverty-stricken parents, and what have you got? That's *the* question at Christmas. What's inside the packaging? What did God want to say in all this? What does God want from us because of it?

Well, if I had to describe the "banana" inside all this Christmas cuteness, it would be this: God loves you — and you — and you. That sounds incredibly trite, doesn't it? Well, that's precisely the problem. Most of us believe that God thinks like Lucy Van Pelt, the Peanuts character. Lucy once said, "I love humanity. It's people I can't stand." We are willing to admit that God loves humanity, but are we willing to accept the fact that God loves me, as I am, with all my mistakes and sins — not when I get better, not when I've paid my dues, but right now?

Instead of mediating this tremendous, unbelievable, and history-piercing good news, organized religion has sometimes obscured it with layer upon layer of "yes buts." It's bad enough that it withholds its blessing from some of its children who have done — or not done — something, but it has gone as far as to bring God's love for them into question. There is a world of difference between disapproving of someone's behavior and actually making them doubt the love God has for them! The "banana" here is that we are purely and simply loved, period.

This dramatic gesture on God's part requires a dramatic response on our part. With God embracing us like this, it is surely not appropriate to turn a cold shoulder. God wants to engage us. Mistakes are understood and easily forgiven. Conversion is not something we do to get God to love us; it's what happens when we wake up to the fact that we have been loved all along. When we really wake up to that fact, changes in behavior will follow. God does not want cringing slaves. He wants to have an affair with us. That's what kind of response God wants: a passionate engagement with you and me, personally. "Make mistakes, get mad at me, disagree with me, but don't ignore me" is what "becoming flesh" was all about!

In the life and worship of our community, we talk about and celebrate this mystery. We'll watch this baby grow up over the next year. We'll hear Jesus describe even more elaborately the madness of God's love.

Scripture Readings

Isaiah 9:1–6
Titus 2:11–14
Luke 2:1–14

Magi: My Kind of People

After Jesus' birth in Bethlehem of Judea during the reign of King Herod, astrologers from the east arrived one day in Jerusalem inquiring, "Where is the newborn king of the Jews? We observed his star at its rising and have come to pay him homage."

— MATTHEW 2:1–2

*T*HE MAGI — the astrologers in Matthew's gospel — are my kind of people. If you think this feast is about a baby shower for Jesus, you've missed the boat. These Magi people are into some heavy-duty looking and searching. They are on a mission.

Who are these characters who would follow some star across strange deserts and mountains, enduring personal risk and unknown danger, listening to dreams and looking for signs? I'll tell you who they are. They are the very opposite of that old woman down in eastern Kentucky I saw interviewed on educational TV. When asked why she had lived her whole life without going more than five miles from where she was born, she answered: "I just don't believe in going places."

Who are these people and what are they looking for? They were originally from a tribe of priests who instructed and taught the kings of Persia. They were good and holy wise men who sought the truth. It was their profession to watch the heavens for something unusual. When they noticed some unusual event in the heavens, they understood that God was announcing something special, as if to say, "And now I interrupt our regular programming to bring you this special announcement."

One star that "acted up" regularly was a star named "the Birth of a Prince." When it acted up, they believed that a great king had been born. There was also a fairly common belief in the East that a Judean king was soon to rule the world. Was this the star they followed? Could that even be happening at that time? The Magi were convinced that it was.

This is no sweet legend. This is one of the things that actually could have happened then. The world was just chomping at the bit for God to come. The world had begun to look for God with intensity. They had finally realized that they would not have a golden age without God. The desire for God was at a fever pitch. This story comes alive when you realize how intense they were in their search.

These are my kind of people. I was in my twenties when I first got "Magi fever." It was then that it first began to dawn on me that life evolves from the inside out rather than the other way around. It was then that I began to realize that I could transform any situation I was in by changing my mind about it. It was then that I began to realize that "heaven" was just a thought away and there was something incredible going on right in front of me if I could just wake up to it. Jesus put it this way: Change the way you see and you will see a kingdom right under your nose. "I was blind but now I see," the wonderful hymn *Amazing Grace* has it.

These are my kind of people. They are driven toward their goal with such determination that nothing can stop them. They were certainly not on a package tour. They were on a mission — an inner quest. Sometimes I believe that we have lost this in the church. Instead of talking people into going on a spiritual adventure, we often just lead religious tours. We give up the goal of transforming people and settle for conformity. If you think taking a tour of shrines of the Holy Land is the same as walking in the footsteps of Jesus, you're not on a spiritual adventure, you're on a package tour. These Magi people were not on a tour. They were on a scary, spiritual adventure — one that took massive amounts of personal courage.

We don't just have a priest shortage, we have a crisis of faith from the top down. Too many of us "just don't believe in going places." There is so much about our church that values keeping people in bounds, constraining the adventurous. We often punish the adventurous and reward, protect, and coddle the mediocre. Just like the Magi, Jesus left his carpenter shop and went on a spiritual adventure. He went about inviting others to drop what they were doing and follow him without looking back.

The solemnity of the Epiphany challenges us to go on a spiritual adventure. It challenges us to consider whether we are going toward something — away from something — or just riding the current. We are asked if we have ever really given our hearts seriously to anything, if we have even identified what is important enough to us to make that commitment. So many of us are *in* things but not *into* them. We're in a marriage; we're priests, parents, parishioners; but we're really not *into* what we're in. There's no intensity, no passion, no fire in our belly.

We don't even have to leave where we are to go on this spiritual adventure. We don't need more money, better health, youth, more favorable times, or more cooperation from people around us. We don't have to trade in our spouses, leave the priesthood, sell the children, or find a new parish. We can go on this quest by changing our attitudes toward what is before us — by deciding to wake up, to find out, to invest some energy and attention, to live on purpose.

If we do decide to live on purpose, to go on a personal and spiritual adventure, we will make unbelievable progress. The more courage, the more progress. But if you go on this adventure, you must also remember that Herods will be lurking in the wings, both inside you and outside you. You will have to confront and stand up to your own resistance and tendency to sabotage yourself, to slip back into feeling comfortable again. You must resist and keep on moving. You will attract fire from others who want you to stay as you are, because your changing upsets their comfort. But you must not let others' discomfort stop you. You can always reassure them as you go, but you must not ask for permission.

There will be temptations to give up along the way. There will be temptations to blame others and find excuses for not moving on, but as Marsha Sinetar observes, when our "desire for a thing we want surpasses our fear of the risk of having it, we realize we can find our way there. When we get tired enough of not having what we want, we'll have no problem deciding what to do! When what we want becomes more powerful than our fear of pain, rejection or criticism, we are ready to do what is necessary!"

Are you ready to let go of your excuses and commit yourself to a spiritual adventure, to follow your star, to go within and find out who you are? Are you tired of living without God? He's in you, waiting to help you, but are you willing to travel inside your own heart — to take possession of your kingdom within? Are you ready to be your own tour guide? If you are, an adventure awaits you. The more courage you have, the more progress you'll make. You have built-in fuel tanks — just switch them on!

Scripture Readings

Isaiah 60:1–6
Ephesians 3:2–3, 5–6
Matthew 2:1–12

Baptism: Your Initiation into Ministry

*After Jesus was baptized, he came directly out of the water.
Suddenly the sky opened, and he saw the Spirit of God...
With that, a voice from the heavens said, "This is my beloved
Son. My favor rests on him."*

— MATTHEW 3:16–17

*T*HE OLD MARBLE BAPTISMAL FONT near the altar in the
Cathedral of the Assumption, where hundreds and hundreds of Catholics were initiated into the Christian faith,
used to be in the back in a chapel, where the elevator is now
located. It was moved forward in 1972. This year we are planning to move it smack dab into the middle aisle. Why has it been
moved so much? Because it looks better here or there? No. It has
been moved because the sacrament of Baptism has been rapidly
regaining its rightful prominence in the Catholic Church in the
last twenty-five years.

Back when this cathedral was built, baptism was touted as important, but many of our actions did not support our claims.
Baptisms were done in Latin, with a thimbleful of stagnant water from a jar kept over from Easter. Baptisms took place so
soon after birth that parents were not even required to attend.
It was done on Sunday afternoon, in the back corner of an empty
church. Usually the only people there were baby, priest, and godparents. They were certainly legal and valid baptisms, but there
wasn't much of a celebration of the sacrament. By 1972, when
this church was last renovated, we were beginning to focus more

on the importance of baptism, so we moved the font up front. By 1993, baptism has become even more prominent in the life of the church. This new location might seem novel to us, but in actuality it is closer to the ancient Christian way of celebrating baptism than either of the other locations.

It's not going to have a sign on it, but because of its location, it will be a teaching symbol for our congregation and those who visit. It will shout, "Baptism is important! This is where we got our start! This is where we were initiated into ministry!" We won't have to explain it. It will speak for itself. And every Sunday, when people come in and dip their hands in its holy water, they'll be reminded like they've never been before that they are baptized members of the church, that they are initiated into the ministry of this church. After a lifetime of ministry in this church, their family and friends will roll their old bones in here so that they can commend them to the Lord. The priest will meet them at the door, pause for a minute at the baptismal font, dip his hands into its water, and sign them one last time with the waters of baptism.

Jesus initiated his public ministry at his baptism in the Jordan River. At his baptism, he received his divine commission to begin his work of opening blind eyes, freeing prisoners, and leading people into the light. Years of brooding, praying, clarifying, and deepening awareness peaked on the banks of the Jordan as Jesus realized that God had a task for him. Lights went on in his head, John's head, and the heads of people around him: God's favor rested on Jesus. Jesus realized it. John realized it. The people around realized it.

You were initiated into that same ministry at your baptism. You were made disciple, ambassador, and representative of Jesus Christ. You also became a chosen, beloved child upon whom God's favor rests. You also were chosen and adopted into God's family at your baptism. Those who have doubts about their infant baptism might remember the blunt words of Jesus: "It was not you who chose me, it was I who chose you" (John 15:16).

But you know, we have a serious problem in the Catholic Church. We have millions of baptized people who haven't the foggiest understanding of what their baptism means. Our new font will not solve this problem. It will, however, be big enough, beautiful enough, noisy enough, and smack-dab-in-the-middle enough to raise a few questions in the minds of people who will confront it head-on every time they enter this church. They may finally understand what the sign of the cross with holy water is all about: a reminder that we are baptized, that God's favor rests upon us, that we have been commissioned to carry on Jesus' ministry.

Maybe it will raise enough questions that some of us will be moved to find out what our baptism means. Maybe it will remind us enough that we are commissioned for ministry, and we will finally get around to doing a bit of opening blind eyes, freeing prisoners, and leading people into the light, literally and figuratively. The church is languishing because we have too many baptized people preoccupied with taking care of themselves and calling it religion. Church is not where you go to be served but where you go to get the strength to serve others.

Baptism is a beginning. It was the beginning of Jesus' ministry. It is the beginning of your ministry. Maybe some of you will find out exactly on what day you were baptized, put it on the calendar each year like you would a birthday, and use it as a time each year to take serious spiritual inventory. It could be the beginning of a whole new spiritual awakening.

Scripture Readings

Isaiah 42:1–4, 6–7
Acts 10:34–38
Matthew 3:13–17

THE PEOPLE
HE LOVED

The Birth of John the Baptist

John the Baptist

He will be filled with the Holy Spirit from his mother's womb. Many of the sons of Israel will he bring back to the Lord their God.

— LUKE 1:15–16

HE HAD A BEARD, so he can't be all bad. But in spite of his beard, John the Baptist has never been one of my favorite saints. Screaming men who wear fur coats and eat bugs make me very nervous. He's not the type of person you could sit out on the deck and have a beer with. Before you could pop the top, he'd be giving you a lecture on the evils of drinking. He has always reminded me of those people who have just gotten back from making a Cursillo or a trip to Medjugorje and can't wait to get in your face and redo your life for you. You know that condescending attitude that says: "I know the truth now and I'm sorry you're so defective." As soon as they start talking, I look for the nearest exit. I've always wanted to say to him: "John, buddy, lighten up!"

But as I have gotten older and wiser, I have begun to appreciate John a little more. In fact, maybe he could be a role model for today's American Catholic. John the Baptist stands out as a believer who is both critical and committed, the two essential ingredients most needed in today's church. He, above all, seems to have found a balance between those two poles.

As our church continues to undergo massive transformation, the tension between the left and the right continues to produce anxiety in the hearts of believers everywhere. It seems that zealots at both ends of the spectrum are claiming to own the truth. Somehow we must cooperate and give up our competition, separatism, and fragments of the truth. Maybe John the Baptist can teach us to ignore zealots of every stripe and listen to the less shrill voices of reason and joy. Maybe we can find some common ground between the hypercritical and the blindly committed. Maybe John can teach us to be both critical and committed.

Criticism, without commitment, is cruelty. There is a growing number of Catholic people who have moved to the edges or left the church altogether to take potshots at the church from their safe positions of smug superiority. They have their well-documented lists of flaws and sins to justify their withdrawal from active church life and are willing to point them out on cue. They are like the people who look at a thorny bush with a single flower and see a thornbush rather than a rosebush. Behind their superior attitude is a belief that others are responsible for the health of the church, and they will not grace the church with their presence until it conforms to their point of view.

Just as dangerous are those who are committed without being critical. Even Pope John Paul II, when he was still Cardinal Wojtyla, wrote in 1969: "Conformism means the death of any community; a loyal opposition is a necessity in any community." Blind commitment without question is also unhealthy for the church. There are those among us who would have us believe that anything our leaders say or do should be followed without question, without hesitation.

Sometimes the church's best friends are those who criticize it. A very respected spiritual writer in our church, Louis Evely, far from being a radical, has written: "The church is dying, and her murderers are those clerics who spend their lives repeating what was said before their time and redoing what was done when they were young. True fidelity is inventive. A faith that asks no questions is not faith. A faith that is not able to put up with questions is not a faith. To have faith means to have enough light to be willing to tolerate certain areas of darkness."

Read church history. Its history is darkest when its prophets were silenced. Prophets challenge too much belief in the status quo. Those who question some of the positions of the church may be its best friends. A case in point: The Vatican defended slavery during the American Civil War. Would disagreement with that position then make you a bad Catholic? Our history is full of cases where we were saved from our own foolishness and cowardice by people who made waves.

Criticism without commitment is cruelty. Commitment without criticism is lazy, sentimental, and infantile. What is needed is the spirit of John the Baptist. He was both critical and committed. What we really need today is people who care enough and love enough to raise some questions. We need committed people who are willing, in the words of Saint Paul, to "profess the truth in love" (Ephesians 4:15). Those who drop out and attack from the outside are no help. Those who stay and bury their heads in blind conformity are dangerous and destructive. What we need is people who are committed but vigilant and attentive, knowing in their hearts that this old church requires, in the words of Pope Paul VI, "that continual reformation of which she always has need." What we need is people who are committed, not to forms and old ways of doing things but to the gospel itself; people who understand that if we are too concerned with preserving our old wineskins, then we shall inevitably lose the new wine.

As a pastor, I am sometimes caught in a tug of war between the critical and the committed. I have tried to model myself after John the Baptist. I have tried to model for you the marriage of those two perspectives. I have tried, especially in my preaching, to be both carefully critical and deeply committed. It's not always a comfortable position, but I believe it is a spiritually healthy position. After all, there is "this treasure we possess in earthen vessels" (2 Corinthians 4:7), and we need to know the difference between the treasure and the crock.

Scripture Readings

JEREMIAH 1:4–10
1 PETER 1:8–12
LUKE 1:5–17

No Boundaries

The Canaanite Woman

"It is not right to take the food of sons and daughters and throw it to the dogs." "Please, Lord," she insisted, "even the dogs eat the leavings that fall from their masters' tables." Jesus then said in reply, "Woman, you have great faith!"
— MATTHEW 15:26–28

DID JESUS get up on the wrong side of the bed, or what? First of all, he snubs a poor woman, pretending not to notice her. When she refuses to take the hint and shut up, his disciples try to gag her. Finally, when Jesus does answer her, he calls her a dog. Undaunted, she hangs in there till she gets what she wants: help for her daughter. This certainly doesn't sound like the Jesus that we all know and love. We all have our bad days, but Jesus too?

It's not as bad as it sounds. In fact, there is some humor here. A lot of what is being said is tongue in cheek. Jesus and this woman are sharing a joke for the benefit of the crowd.

First of all, Jesus had left Jewish territory for the first time. He went there on a retreat of sorts. There was no place in Palestine where he could be assured privacy and he knew that no Jew would follow him into this foreign country. But his reputation had spread even beyond Jewish borders. A foreign woman begs for help. All eyes are on Jesus. Would he help her? After all, she is a woman, she is a non-Jew, and worse, she is a Canaanite — an enemy of the Jews. Here stands Jesus with a crying Gentile woman in need on one hand and a group of people with narrow ideas about God on the other — ideas like women are inferior, God only loves Jews, and all foreigners are trash.

To understand this passage correctly, you have to imagine Jesus and the woman teasing and winking at each other as they talk. Imagine Jesus winking at her and saying, "Hey, you're a woman! You know what they say: 'Jewish men don't give women the time of day, much less foreign women.'" Imagine Jesus winking at her and saying, "Hey, you're a foreigner — a dog, remember? You know what they say, 'God only cares about Jews.' It isn't right to take goodies meant for the children of Abraham and give them to Gentile dogs like yourself." Imagine the woman, picking up on the joke, winking back, and saying, "Well, sir, even little puppies like me would be willing to settle for a few crumbs from their master's table." The story ends with the woman getting what she wanted.

This story is significant in that it signals the end of all barriers to God's love. The old walls, the old rules, the old prejudices, the old categories all melt away with Jesus. The gospel will close with the disciples being sent out to the whole world to proclaim God's universal love. In Christ there is no "Jew or Greek, slave or freeman, male or female" (Galatians 3:28). God's love knows no bounds. God is on everybody's side, especially the poor and outcast. God does not accept our categories, boundaries, pigeonholes, and classes. God's love includes everybody.

During the Apollo mission in 1969, Rusty Sweikert was let out of the capsule on an umbilical cord. Something went wrong and he was left floating outside the capsule for a long time. While he floated in space, he had a religious experience. He looked down on Mother Earth and saw no boundaries, just one beautiful world hanging there like a "beautiful gem against a black backdrop." He realized that nations exist only in the minds of human beings. All the boundaries, classes, and categories are created by human beings. He saw the world from God's perspective: beautiful and whole in all its variety. For six months after he returned, he was in a stupor, contemplating over and over again what he had experienced. He got to see the world as God sees it.

God created variety and called it good and beautiful, but we have always been afraid of it. It has always threatened us. Instead of appreciating difference, seeing its beauty, we have always resorted to attempts to convert, control, force, crush, ridicule, stereotype, discriminate, shun, excommunicate, isolate, and manipulate those who are different from the majority. In short, we have tried to mold everything to our own image, likeness, and taste. Instead of appreciating all the variety and difference, the nations of the world spend a million dollars a minute protecting themselves against the differences. If we could ever discover a healthy respect for variety, we would discover the way to world peace. Our tired old definition of unity as uniformity not only doesn't work, it has been the driving force behind untold violence against the variety that God himself created. We desperately need a new definition of unity — not only in the church but in the world too — that embraces and reconciles variety. The solution is to celebrate, not obliterate, our individual and cultural differences.

Jesus did not tell us we had to like everybody, but that we must love everybody. That means we have to be big enough to go beyond our fears and not be controlled by them. Love is not about feeling good; it's about unconditional acceptance and reverence for everybody — even our enemies. Even if they strike us on one cheek, we must turn the other.

We all have the power to bless others. To bless people does not mean to wave a cross over them. It means to accept and affirm others as acceptable just the way they are — to believe in your heart that it's OK to be Muslim, Jewish, black, yellow, Indian, conservative, or liberal; that it's OK to speak a different language, to eat different foods, to dance different dances, to have different values and tastes. The world will always be a dangerous place until we learn to appreciate difference. We often say, "Variety is the spice of life," but when will we really believe it enough to live it?

We all need to trade in our one-eyed points of view for a vantage point where we can appreciate many points of view. We need to see each other as God sees us. We don't need to go up in a space capsule to do that. We can do it by choosing today to bless all people, no matter how different they are, and by choosing today to cease demanding that all people conform to our point of view. We can choose to reverence all people — Arabs, Jews, Hindus, Protestants, Catholics, blacks, whites, reds, yellows, young people, old people, women, men, the handicapped, Asians, conservatives, radicals, atheists, street people, millionaires, and everyone in between. We have a planet full of people with points of view trying to neutralize other people's points of view, sometimes violently. Why not move to a vantage point that will help us appreciate not only our own point of view but other points of view? We are varied by God's design, and so we need to use our resources and imagination to find an agreeable way to disagree. It may save the world.

If Jesus could embrace sinners without approving of their sins, why are we so afraid to embrace each other? Why does difference have to be a cause of hostility? I think our mission, to include as many as we can, is something we ought to be proud of. What we learn here, what we construct here, can mold us into more tolerant people. We can begin by leaving our sexism, racism, homophobia, and ageism at the door. Then from our little corner of the world we can go out and be a leaven of tolerance and respect in the world outside these walls. Blessed are the peacemakers!

Scripture Readings

ISAIAH 56:1, 6–7
ROMANS 11:13–15, 29–32
MATTHEW 15:21–28

Blind Trust

Peter

So Peter got out of the boat and began to walk on the water, moving toward Jesus. But when he perceived how strong the wind was, becoming frightened, he began to sink and cried out, "Lord, save me!"

— MATTHEW 14:29–30

*I*MAGINE YOURSELF for a minute as Jesus watching Peter come toward you across the water, with panic-stricken eyes and begging for help. I've often wondered what Peter's face looked like to Jesus at that moment. I believe I know exactly what it was like. I've watched someone drowning close-up.

It was the summer of 1959. I was barely fourteen years old, and it was my first summer home from the seminary. It was a Sunday afternoon. My brother and I and two other boys from our small town of Rhodelia rode our bicycles to my dad's farm pond about three miles away. None of us could swim very well, so we played together along the shore, taking turns clinging to one old inner tube. At least I thought we were all together. All of a sudden, from across the pond, came a blood-curdling scream for help. Joe-Joe was drowning! My brother and I barely managed to paddle ourselves across the pond. His brother got out of the water and ran around the shore. By the time my brother and I got to him, we were almost drowning ourselves. Right before my eyes, no more than four feet away, my friend and neighbor stared a riveting, pleading stare right into my eyes, right into my soul, as he went down for the last time. An hour later, the Meade County

Sheriff dragged his blue-gray body onto the shore as my brother and I watched in horror.

The story in Matthew's gospel is not just about Jesus saving Peter from physical drowning. If it were only that we might be "wowed" by Jesus' power for a few minutes, but it wouldn't have a thing to do with us today. This story has been preserved and told to us through the centuries because it teaches us something about a deeper kind of drowning: spiritual and emotional drowning. The best thing I have seen recently to describe this other kind of drowning is a "children's movie for adults." *The Neverending Story* is about a little boy who finds himself as the central character on a hero's journey in a book he is reading. The movie depicts his struggle to keep the faith when everyone around him in the kingdom is giving in to the Nothing that is devouring the land. In one of my favorite scenes, his horse gets mired in the Swamps of Sadness. Reaching out to him from the shore, the young hero pleads with his beautiful white horse: "Don't give in to the sadness! Don't give in to the sadness!" He is really saying the same thing that Jesus said to Peter: "Don't give in to your doubt, Peter! Don't quit believing, no matter how bad it gets!" In the movie, the panic-stricken horse is soon swallowed up in the quicksand of sadness. I've often thought that if my drowning childhood buddy had only known how to relax and had not given in to his fear and panic, he might have saved his own life. He might have floated, or my brother and I might have pulled him the few feet to shore.

When this gospel was written, huge and terrible storms had beset the church during the persecutions under Nero. Remembering this story brought comfort and strength to the church in terrible times. The early Christians felt very much like Peter out on the water and going under. Remembering this story reminded them that Jesus always came when their limits had been reached. Like Peter out on the water, they realized that they sank only when their eyes wavered, when they gave in to their terror and doubt, when they took their eyes off Jesus and realized how strong the winds were and how deep the water was. By focusing on Jesus — and remembering this story — they found themselves doing the impossible. They found themselves "walking on water," and somehow they managed to survive.

This is not just a treasured and hope-filled story for the early church. It contains a teaching for those of us who hear it again. Some of you have walked on water. You have survived terrible storms: health, relationships, and personal loss. As I was writing these words, I thought of the heroic people along the flooding Mississippi River, the residents of Sarajevo, and the many people who barely manage to exist in the inner cities across this country. What keeps them from giving up? What keeps them treading water? Some of you are walking on water right now, handling difficult situations one day at a time. Some of you are in recovery from various addictions. Some of you are grieving the loss of a loved one, perhaps a child. Some of you are living with chronic pain, and still others are fighting off the bitterness that can move into a person's heart after acute disappointment. Maybe you don't even know how you're doing it, but you do it one day at a time. You're walking on water.

My friends, sometimes we find ourselves out in deep water without warning. It only takes a few words and a few seconds: "The biopsy is malignant." "The results of your blood test reveal that you are HIV positive." "Your new baby has some major birth defects." "Honey, the plant is closing." "Mom, you are going to have to go to a nursing home." "I don't love you anymore. I want a divorce." "Father, the walls of the cathedral are cracking." Statements such as these bring on paralyzing fear and distress. But these are also invitations to trust, invitations to walk on water. They bring overwhelming temptations to give up and give in to hopelessness and despair. It takes faith — it always has — lots and lots of faith to walk on water.

We must nourish our faith if it is to serve us in times of crisis. It's one thing to worship God. It's another to trust God. It's very easy to go to church, even on a regular basis. It is another thing to pierce the darkness of despair and keep trusting God in the darkest moments of life. It is not what happens to you in life that is truly important, but how you react to it. In that sense, our faith can save us.

Are you nurturing the kind of faith required to walk on water if need be? That's one of the reasons we gather for worship: to nourish our faith. Let us be intentional about it. Let's learn to trust God at every moment of our lives, not only when things are going right, but especially when we feel like we're going under. God is our bridge over troubled water. And it is Jesus who stretches out his hand to hold us.

Scripture Readings

1 KINGS 19:9, 11–13
ROMANS 9:1–5
MATTHEW 14:22–33

Fear vs. Trust

The Woman with a Hemorrhage

Fear is useless. What is needed is trust.
— MARK 5:36

BEING A PRIEST is a privilege. There are certain moments that one never forgets, no matter how many years go by.

A few years ago I was called to a hospital to visit an eleven-year-old boy who was just brought in with critical burns all over his body. In fact, the only places not burned were the tips of his fingers and the bottoms of his feet. He and his friend had lit a match while playing on a gas tank. In the explosion, his friend was killed outright. About all the doctors could do was to wrap the burns, sedate the boy, and wait. There was no skin to graft.

I made several visits over a ten-day period. One night I went in and the nurses were in tears. They told me that since the bandages could not be removed, they believed that the boy was literally rotting under the bandages, maybe even that maggots had begun to grow. But his heart was still strong and they believed that he could go on living for several more days.

The family had surrounded the boy all week, whispering words of encouragement, telling him to hang on. The nurses advised me to go on home. I remembered something I had read in pastoral counseling. I went into the room, took a deep swallow, and went to the head of the bed. Then I turned around and said to the family, "You have shown all week that you truly love Johnny. You have told him to hang in there. He has been trying to do as you say. Maybe it's time to tell him it's OK to let go."

They looked at each other and nodded approval. Beginning with the grandmother, all of them — parents, brothers, and sisters — came to the head of the bed and began to pat his head and stroke his bandaged arms. They told him how brave he had been, how hard he had tried, how much they loved him, and that it was all right to let go and that God would take care of him. As each one came forward, I finally had to leave and give them their privacy.

I was standing outside the room with the nurse. In about fifteen minutes, the nurse said, "I can't believe this!" The numbers on his monitor had begun to fall, little by little. In less than a half hour, the poor little boy died, surrounded by his family.

It proved to me how responsive the body is to the mind. This is something Jesus knew very well in his healing ministry. Even though it needed to work in reverse in this situation, Jesus knew that a positive attitude of faith can heal and a negative attitude of fear can kill.

In Mark's gospel story of the woman with the hemorrhage, Jesus is surrounded with both positive thinking and negative thinking, surrounded with both trust and fear. This prompts him to come out with this gem of wisdom: "Fear is useless. What is needed is trust." Jairus, the synagogue official, goes public with his trust. Risking his reputation, he goes to Jesus for help, believing that Jesus has the power to heal his daughter. His associates and friends are filled with negative thoughts: mistrust, despair, and ridicule. The woman with the hemorrhage is filled with trust and faith, but she takes the back door. She sneaks up behind Jesus, believing that she can get her cure and get away unnoticed. The disciples are filled with hopelessness, despair, and negative thinking. So we see, in this story within a story, trust and fear side by side. Jesus is confronted with both. Those with faith and trust get better; those filled with despair are dumbfounded. "Fear is useless. What is needed is trust." "It is your faith that has cured you."

"Fear is useless. What is needed is trust." I just love it, because I have finally come to know how true it is. Fear seems to be epidemic in our society. We fear beginnings. We fear endings. We fear changing. We fear being stuck. We fear success. We fear failure. We fear living. We fear dying. But Jesus says to us that fear is useless — trust is needed. Just as the people who surrounded Jesus in the gospel story were stuck in a mindset of hopelessness, despair, "nothing can be done–ism," and negativity, so too are many of us. Just as two people in the reading stepped out of that negativity, trusted, and were healed, so can we. "Fear is useless. What is needed is trust."

Notice the words Jesus used when he spoke to the woman after her cure: "It is your faith that has cured you." Fascinating words! He did not say "I cured you." No, he said, "It is your faith that has cured you." I am reminded of another passage in the gospels. It refers to Jesus' inability to work many cures in Nazareth: "He did not work many miracles there because of their lack of faith" (Matthew 13:58). There is nothing more powerful than a closed mind. Even God seems stymied by a closed and negative mind. Any doctor can tell you that there is very little that can be done for a person who does not have the will to live.

In my study of the ministry of Jesus, I have concluded that what he did primarily was attack the negative thinking that produced so many negative circumstances. Once he did that, he triggered the natural healing power in people — spiritually, physically, and emotionally. Look what he did for Mary Magdalene. Look at every miracle that took place. He started with faith and trust. Without that, even he was powerless. "Fear is useless." (Fear is negative thinking.) "What is needed is trust." (Trust is positive thinking.) Peter sinks when he thinks about sinking but walks on water when he trusts. Bread is multiplied when people trust they will have enough. Water is turned into wine when Mary says with confidence: "Do whatever he tells you." Blind people see, cripples walk, the dead are raised to life — all when trust and faith are unleashed. The demons that Jesus cast out were negative thought patterns that caused so much suffering in the lives of the people around him.

I am often amazed these days at what psychologists are just now discovering and calling "new," things that Jesus was evidently aware of nearly two thousand years ago and expressed in so many wonderful ways that are recorded in Holy Scripture. "Fear is useless. What is needed is trust." "Whatever you ask for in prayer with faith, you will receive" (Matthew 21:22). Our thoughts are like seed. As you sow, so shall you reap. Thoughts will take root and produce. If those thoughts are bad, bad will be the results. If those thoughts are good, good will be the results. If we are filled with fear and mistrust, we will reap a harvest of suffering. If we are filled with trust and confidence, we will reap a harvest of rich blessings. "Give and gifts will be given to you; . . . packed together, shaken down and overflowing, they will be poured out into the folds of your garment. The measure with which you measure will be measured out to you" (Luke 6:32).

Most of us do not know how powerful we are in directing our lives. We speak of luck and fate. We have not yet seen the connection between our thinking and its results, the circumstances around us. We are unhappy, but we don't know why. What we do not know is that most of our misery is self-inflicted. It is the result of negative thinking, of fear, and anxiety. "Fear is useless. What is needed is trust." Anxiety, fear, and mistrust are mental attitudes that produce anything from heart disease to loneliness. Both fear and trust produce results. The only difference is that fear is useless and trust triggers healing and wholeness.

We have a choice. Our lives will — indeed, already do — result from the choices we make: "I have set before you life and death, the blessing and the curse. Choose life, then, that you . . . may live" (Deuteronomy 30:19). Jesus did not come to change things but to change minds. "Repent!" he said. "The kingdom of God is at hand. It is within you!" (Matthew 10:6; Luke 17:20). Change the way you think, and the world will be changed for you and by you.

Scripture Readings

WISDOM 1:13–15, 2:23–24
2 CORINTHIANS 8:7, 9, 13–15
MARK 5:21–43

A Story of Worth

Martha and Mary of Bethany

*Martha, Martha, you are anxious and upset about many
things; one thing only is required.*

— LUKE 10:41–42

BECAUSE I DIDN'T REALLY UNDERSTAND IT, I never liked
the Martha/Mary story very much. In fact, I believed that
Martha got a bum deal here. Here she is slaving away in
a hot kitchen, trying to get a meal on the table, while her sister
Mary has parked herself in the living room with the guests, listening in on all the chitchat. And even when poor Martha comes
into the living room, mopping her brow with her apron, to ask
for a little help, she not only doesn't get it, but she also gets a
quick reprimand for being such a workaholic.

To the best of my understanding, Jesus is not condemning good
deeds or hard work in order to praise contemplation. In the sequence of the gospel, Jesus has just finished telling the story of
the Good Samaritan, in which good deeds are praised. In fact,
Jesus ends that story by telling his disciples, and us, to go and do
the same. What he is doing here is simply reminding Martha of
the primacy of listening to the Lord and also reminding her why
and for whom she is doing all this work to begin with. So this
story is meant to balance the story of the Good Samaritan. It's
not a matter of either/or but of both/and. It's a matter of action
and contemplation.

Now I suppose this story can be read on many levels. In fact,
in the twentysomething years that I have preached on this text, it

has spoken to me on a variety of levels, depending on where I was in my own experience. But last week when I picked it up and read it two or three times, all of a sudden it took on a new meaning. As I read it over and over, I kept saying to myself: "This story is about self-worth. This is about self-worth!"

I know these two women. They have moved into my head and they have been arm-wrestling for years over who is going to be in charge of my thinking. For most of my life I've sided with the busy and anxious Martha. But recently, as I've gotten older, Martha is really getting on my nerves. Mary, after all, is the smart one. Both of these characters want to serve the Lord, but they do it for different reasons. Martha is that part of me that believes that I am not really worth much unless I do a lot. Martha is that part of me that is always anxious, always lecturing myself, saying that I ought to be ashamed of myself for not being perfect. Martha is that part of me that believes that if I accomplish a lot, then maybe I can make up for my deficiencies. Martha is that side of me that believes that my worth is directly tied into what I can do. If you have a Martha in your head, I am sure you are totally exhausted most of the time by your busyness about many things.

I've just recently discovered Mary's point of view. Mary knows that she is already loved, and so she doesn't have to do a thing about it except enjoy it. Mary is that side of me that wants to believe that God already loves me, no matter what, just as I am right now, and whether I do anything this week or not. Mary is that part of me that wants to believe that God loves me and I am worth something just because I am, not because I am a priest or I've earned a few degrees or I've done this or that. Martha always leaves me anxious, and Mary leaves me encouraged and she gives me mental rest. Martha is always trying to do something to get God to love her, and Mary understands that she is already loved.

Now many of us grew up believing that God's love is conditional. Therefore, we had to do certain things, and refrain from doing other things, in order to prove worthy of God's love. We had to belong to the right denomination, know the correct beliefs, and perform the proper rituals in order to get God to love us. Well, that might be good, and it is certainly good for a religious organization, but it is very poor theology. God's love for humankind does not have to be earned. True, God may not approve of all our actions and behaviors, and certainly God does let us reap what we sow, but God never withholds love from us, no matter what we do.

Our church has had a chronic case of "Martha-itis" for many, many years. This disease has compromised the earth-shaking good news of God's unconditional love. Because we have this disease, we are always "conditionalizing" that message — almost out of existence. No wonder people are yawning in churches these days. The powder has been taken out of the dynamite. Instead of mediating this tremendous, unbelievable message, the church essentially obscures it with layer upon layer of "God loves you, *but...*" The church must be held accountable for the conditions it places on God's mercy.

Disapproving of people's actions or omissions should never be an excuse for implying that God's love for them is in doubt. That's inexcusable. Its flat-out evil. Besides, it doesn't work. People turn around in their lives through love and acceptance, not through harsh condemnation. Conversion, as I have said hundreds of times, is not something that we go through to get God to love us. Conversion comes on that day, in that hour, when we realize for the first time that God has loved us all along. By withholding its blessing from some people, the church steps out of preaching conversion and ends up wanting the shortcut of external conformity. That's loving the earthenware jar rather than the great treasure that it contains. If this is happening, then our teachers need to be converted, because if they themselves have not felt this unconditional love and discovered this buried treasure, then they will continue to do incredible damage to good people in the name of religion.

My friends, our world is crowded with people who are self-doubting and feel unloved even by their God. And because they feel unloved, they roam through our streets and cities and families desperately looking for love, often in some terrible places. More often than not, they end up settling for painkillers rather than genuine love. Barbara Jordan quoted an African proverb recently on network television. She said it takes a village to raise a child. Yet many children in this country grow up without even one person to model love for them and to teach them how worthwhile they are, while hundreds model hate and teach them to doubt their own worth. Even the church has contributed to their self-doubt by going so far as to call into question God's love for them.

In the last few years, the Cathedral of the Assumption has seen incredible growth. Because I carry the title of pastor, sometimes I receive a lot of credit. But it is not due to me. It's not due to the staff or the musicians. I believe that it's due to the message, and that's why I discourage applause for homilies in Catholic churches. All of this affirmation for the message might get transferred to the messenger. And rather than reflect the Light, he might start absorbing it. Although I preach the message, the preacher is not the message. The staff has worked hard, and we have celebrated and modeled the unconditional love of God for a lot of people who have never experienced it. We have welcomed anybody who wants to come here, and many do come, from miles around. People are not starving for Ron Knott, but for some good news. My role is to induce a process that will change Marthas into Marys, where more people will realize that they are already loved by God just as they are. If only the church would model its own words in the Eucharistic Prayer: "When we were lost and could not find our way to you, you loved us more than ever" (Eucharistic Prayer for Masses of Reconciliation I). If we did that as a church, we would be thriving everywhere.

My friends, you are worthy, not because some church leader has granted it to you, but simply because of who you are. May God forgive our church for its constant message that women, the divorced, gays, ex-Catholics, and those who dare to ask questions are somehow defective and therefore deserve to have our blessing withheld from them. You are worthy because of who you are, not because of some opinion poll.

You are worthy. You are already loved. Yes, you can refuse it. Other people may try to cause you to doubt it. But neither you nor they can stop it. God has made up his mind on this, and there is no changing it. God is love and this is the gospel. This is precisely what kept Mary spellbound. And this is why Jesus wanted Martha to come out of her busy kitchen and sit down and hear it: Martha, you're already loved, even if you don't get dinner on the table.

Scripture Readings

GENESIS 18:1–10
COLOSSIANS 1:24–28
LUKE 10:38–42

God's Tears

Martha, Mary, and Lazarus

When Jesus saw [Mary] weeping and the Jews who had accompanied her also weeping, he was troubled in spirit, moved by the deepest emotions. . . . Jesus began to weep.
— JOHN 11:33–35

LONELINESS is a priest's biggest enemy. If it's not faced squarely, it will bring even the best to ruin. I believe that this is what is behind all the sick and destructive behavior that we read about and hear about almost every day now. If we priests don't deal with it in a healthy way, it will continue to kill us one way or another: emotionally, professionally, spiritually, or physically. Lucky is the priest who has a place to let down his hair, a place where he can be nothing but himself. But such places are as scarce as hen's teeth. For Jesus, it was the home of Martha, Mary, and Lazarus in the village of Bethany. It was his emotional watering hole. From the gospels we know that he went there often.

I had such a place in the little village of Calvary in rural Kentucky. Right down from the church and rectory lived a wonderful Martha of a woman named Dorothy Spalding and her three brothers: Bernard, Benny, and Edward. The reason I gravitated toward their house is that none of them had ever married. It was a home away from home. I always felt welcome. I was always fed. And after a few hours, I always went home to my big old empty rectory refreshed and renewed. They took the edge off that extreme loneliness and isolation that especially afflicts young country pastors. It was my emotional watering hole.

If you pay attention to the details of John's gospel story about Martha, Mary, and Lazarus, you soon realize just how close Jesus was to these people. This is a story about intimate friends, affectionate friends. First of all, we know that this Mary might be the Mary who kissed Jesus' feet in public, washing them with her tears, drying them with her hair, and rubbing them with perfumed oil. (When was the last time anybody kissed your feet?!) Where does Jesus turn in the face of his impending death? He heads straight for their house. Read down the text and you see that John underlines again and again just how intimate they were with Jesus: "Lord, the one you love is sick." "Jesus loved Martha and her sister and Lazarus very much." "See how much he loved him!" They are even so close that these two women can "chew him out" and get away with it: "Lord, if you had been here, my brother would never have died." And finally, seeing Mary weep, we are told that "Jesus began to weep," too.

One usually thinks of this story as the "raising of Lazarus," but Jesus' raising of Lazarus actually occupies a very small part of this story. Of the forty-four verses that constitute this story, only seven of them take place at Lazarus's tomb. The miracle of the raising of Lazarus is the climax of this story; it is not the center. This is a dialogue between Jesus and the two women about God's power in life.

In his gospel, John's stories always have two levels: one on the surface which is true and another below the surface which is truer still. This intimate story is meant to reveal to us not only the depth of their friendship, but also how intimate is God's relationship with us. The pain of this family is the pain of God for his people. By listening in to the dialogue, we are also taught what they were taught: about the depth of God's love for us, about God's willingness to give us new life, and about God's power over our worst enemy — death.

We are taught about the depths of God's love for us. One of the biggest challenges I have faced as a priest is to convince people of God's unconditional love for them. Why is it that so many of us have been trained by people who have dismissed these intimate stories of God's love and have combed through the Scriptures, piecing together condemning, judging, and damning messages that they turn into a religion? Why did they, and why do we, find these messages more believable? I have received more letters questioning my "too lenient notions of God's love" than any other critical letters since I became a priest. Jesus revealed the "true God," not this "false god" that we have created since Adam and Eve. In that story, God says to Adam and Eve, "Who told you that you were naked?" (Genesis 3:11). In other words, "Who told you that you were bad, separated from me, and defective? I certainly didn't!" Jesus came to talk us out of the mean God we keep creating in our own minds. This story is meant to tell us that even death loses its power in Jesus. Eternal life is available, not only after our death, but right now. Death is not final.

By listening in on the conversation of Jesus, Martha, and Mary, we are taught also about God's willingness to give us new life. This eternal life is on both sides of death. Death does not have the last word. Eternal life is not just some promise for the future; it is available to us right now. Through Jesus and in Jesus, those of us who are "dead on our feet" can be resurrected now. We can be born again. We can act boldly on our own behalf to live purposeful lives, to help others, and to claim the powers that lie dormant within us. One of my favorite old movies is *Harold and Maude*. This is Maude's message to Harold throughout the movie: Oh, how the world dearly loves a cage! There are a lot of people who enjoy being dead.

And as this gospel teaches us, God has power over our worst enemy — death. We live in a death-denying culture. Some of our expensive funeral practices would leave outsiders with the impression that we believe that we are going to come up with a cure for it some day. That makes about as much sense as leaving the runway lights on for Amelia Earhart. We don't even know how to die. Modern medical technology can do wonderful things, but it also sometimes robs us of the spiritual experience of "letting go" of this part of our life. Through Jesus and in Jesus, we are able to see in death that "life is changed, not ended." I feel sorry for those who are conscious at death's door without any faith.

This year I have had the awesome privilege of talking to two very conscious people getting ready to die, one with AIDS and another with cancer. Neither was a pious person, but both were deeply spiritual. Both told me that they accepted their approaching deaths and they wanted to "do it well." Both were extremely thankful for the "eternal life" they had experienced in this world. Both looked with "joyful hope" for the "eternal life" ahead of them. You know, it doesn't get any better than that. I hope I can do half as well.

The message is this: God loves you very, very much. He wants you to enjoy the eternal life that you experience right now, and he wants you to know that death does not have the last word. You can have this "eternal life" forever.

Scripture Readings

EZEKIEL 37:12–14
ROMANS 8:8–11
JOHN 11:1–45

Worth Dropping Everything For

Peter, Andrew, James, and John

On the sabbath [Jesus] entered the synagogue and began to teach. The people were spellbound by his teaching because he taught with authority.

— MARK 1:21–22

WHAT WOULD CAUSE four grown men to walk out of their family businesses and follow a man with a message? One of two things is going on here. Either they are completely naive or the message is simply irresistible. Can you imagine something so convincing that you are moved to simply walk away from your old life and begin a new one? That's what happened in Mark's gospel story of four fishermen named Peter, Andrew, James, and John. They met a man with a message — Jesus of Nazareth — who said, "Come after me; I will make you fishers of men." What was their response? They dropped everything and followed him. Later we find Jesus delivering that same message from a synagogue pulpit to the people of Capernaum. What was their response? "The people were spellbound by his teaching because he taught with authority, and not like the scribes."

I was suspicious of the word *spellbound*, so I called Sister Marylee King of Spalding University, a parishioner of the Cathedral of the Assumption, to ask her about it. Sure enough, it isn't a good translation. The crowds were not "eating it up." They were not "spellbound." Rather, they were astounded, bewildered, and incensed. Unlike other rabbis who were always saying, "The Scriptures say," this rabbi was saying, "I say!" The crowds, in contrast to Peter, Andrew, James, and John, were shocked by his message.

What did Jesus say that turned four fishermen into disciples and turned the crowd off? "The reign of God is at hand! Reform your lives and believe in the gospel!" (Mark 1:15). That's it. That is the kernel of the Christian message. If those words are so important and so powerful, what do they mean?

There are three things here: (1) "the reign of God is at hand," (2) "reform your lives," and (3) "believe in the gospel."

1. "The reign of God is at hand!" Another way to put it is: God has intervened in history; the old days of punishment and judgment are over; a new era of mercy and love has begun. From here on out, Jesus, God in the flesh, will emphasize not the sin of the sinner but the mercy and love of God. Awareness of this love will change the hearts of sinners and they will be moved to change their behavior. The authentic Christian message calls, above all, for a change of heart—a radical, internal change of the person. If a person changes his or her heart, then his or her actions will follow. The problem we face is this: Very few Christians understand this because their teachers don't really believe it.

2. "Reform your lives." The original Greek word for "reform" is *metanoia*. The translation here is "reform your lives." The word is rendered "repent" in other translations. In my estimation, both "reform" and "repent" miss the point. *Metanoia* means more than giving up sinful habits or making a few adjustments in one's behavior. We can't just put a few patches on the old cloak; the old cloak has got to go. It's worn out. God's loving intervention in history requires not just a few behavioral adjustments, but a total transformation of the basic structures and style of one's life—similar to a caterpillar becoming a butterfly. This new era will require a new kind of person!

3. "Believe in the gospel!" If Jesus ushered in a new age in

which the love and mercy of God are emphasized and punishment and judgment are de-emphasized, an age when we are invited to believe the good news, the gospel, then why is religion still cranking out so much bad news? Both liberals and conservatives have failed us. Conservatives are still into patching the old garment, still trying to fix the old by editing new editions of the old rules, still trying to fix it from the outside, still trying to control behaviors. Liberals have missed the point as well. They too want to fix it from the outside, to make changes without ever personally changing. They want to stay caterpillars and simply dress up like butterflies. They want to feel good without being good. Both are cranking out bad news. Neither has believed the good news or has understood the new era.

I suppose I have a reputation for being more in the liberal camp than in the conservative camp. I have tried to preach the good news year in and year out: Everybody is loved, everybody is accepted, everybody is welcome. Some have misinterpreted "We welcome everyone" as meaning "Anything goes." As a result I am taking a few kicks in the teeth when I have had to say "no" to "Anything goes."

Both liberals and conservatives have tended to treat people as children — one too permissive and the other too abusive. Jesus announced a new era, an era of God's tremendous unconditional love. But he also required an era of transformed people. This new era requires a change of heart that leads to a change of behavior. Our old ways of living are killing us; our old religious behaviors are not working; our old attitudes and dispositions must change. We cannot keep making liberal or conservative changes. My friends, *we* have to change! This change has to be made from the inside out, one person at a time. This change is triggered and made possible by believing in the good news that Jesus brought to the world. You cannot "believe in the gospel" and not go through the necessary personal transformation any more than a caterpillar can become a butterfly without going through the necessary metamorphosis.

I suppose it is the same now as it was in the beginning — the good news will turn some people on and some people off. I suppose the job of the preacher is to give people a chance to make their response by making it clear what the choices are and then letting the chips fall where they may. As always, some will hate the messenger as well as the message, while some will respond and produce a hundredfold.

Scripture Readings

JONAH 3:1–5, 10
1 CORINTHIANS 7:29–31
MARK 1:14–22

A Little Bit of
Everybody in All of Us
The Sinner at Prayer

I give you thanks, O God, that I am not like the rest of men.
— LUKE 18:11

"**H**YPOCRITES" UP FRONT, the "humble" in the rear — that's how seating arrangements went when I was growing up. At least that's what we thought. The rich, the uppity, and the well-educated sat toward the front. Drunks, the poor, and the insecure, in all their marvelous country-parish variety, staked out the back seats. Nobody made us sit that way, but that was the pecking order. Families sat in the same locations, generation after generation. Even though there were no names on the pews, we knew where people were "supposed" to sit. God help you if you dared sit elsewhere! Stares would focus on you with all the intensity of a laser beam. We exercised great control over each other. Anyone who was ever raised in a small town knows exactly what I mean by that.

My family, characteristically, chose the middle — dead center, in fact. After all, we considered ourselves better than some people and not as good as others. That's how we felt, and that's how we sat. We were also a bit ambivalent toward God: We were neither too close to him nor too far away. We followed the rules, but we were never accused of being religious fanatics. We chose a safe distance. We were a lot like the religiously ambivalent woman in *The Color Purple*: "It ain't easy, trying to do without God.

Even if you know he ain't there, trying to do without him is a strain."

Now all of you who choose front seats in the church need not panic. Neither holiness nor the effectiveness of one's prayer has anything to do with where you sit in church, or whether you go to church for that matter. It has to do with one's attitude toward God and neighbor. It's in the heart and not in the seating location. The parable of the Pharisee and the publican is about attitudes in prayer, not about where you park your body.

> Two men went up to the temple to pray.... [One] went home...justified but the other did not.

The first man — the Pharisee — a meticulously religious man, knew of his success in keeping rules and knew of the failure of others to do the same. He was proud of his success and contemptuous of those who were not so successful. When he approached God, he not only proceeded to inform God just how good he was, but also compared his grocery list of spiritual successes to that of the man in the back: He thanked God he wasn't "grasping, crooked, adulterous" — or even like this tax collector. He knew he could be good without God's help, if necessary. He was self-righteous.

The second man — the publican — aware of his failures, simply asked for God's forgiveness and acceptance. He knew he needed God's love and forgiveness, because he was aware of his inability to be good on his own power. He compared himself to no one but God and was humbled.

Often when we read the parables, we tend to identify the good and the bad, winners and losers, and the hypocrites and the humble — as if reality fell into two simple categories. Then, when we believe we have identified the villain, we project it on to others. We condemn in others what we really hate in ourselves. This condemnation makes it easy to believe that we are really different — better and more favored by God. Homophobic people, for instance, have this mental process down to an art. Maybe we ought to read this parable as if *both* of these characters exist in all of us. In truth, there is a part of both in each of us. Instead of condemning in others what we do not want to see in ourselves, let us "own" the Pharisee within us.

The Pharisee in all of us exists in our conscious mind. We would like to believe that we are "not like the rest" of humanity — "grasping, crooked, adulterous" — when in actuality we really are like the rest of humanity. We would like to believe that we are better, different, and even more favored by God. We select out of the truth what we want to believe about ourselves and project the rest on to a convenient list of the grasping, crooked, and adulterous. Instead of owning it, we project it on to others and disown it.

After we condemn them, we invoke God's condemnation of them as well. When God doesn't join us in our condemnation, we pout like Jonah, like the older son, like the vineyard workers who worked all day, and like the Pharisees. Jonah pouted because God was so forgiving. He wanted the Ninevites "fried in hell." The "older son" pouted outside the house because the father was so forgiving. He wanted his brother punished. The vineyard workers who put in a full day pouted because the latecomers were paid the same as they were. They wanted more for themselves and less for the others. The Pharisees pouted because Jesus was a friend of sinners, welcomed them, and ate with them. They wanted Jesus to do what they did — condemn and exclude. The Pharisee in all of us resents God taking away our delight in having "sinners" punished. In theology courses in my seminary days, we used to call it the sin of morose delectation — taking delight in others' failures.

The publican also exists in all of us — in our subconscious mind, where we store those things that we do not like to see about ourselves, where we store that information that we do not want to own. Down deep we know that there is a little Jim Bakker, Richard Nixon, Donald Trump, Adolf Hitler, and Pharisee in all of us, no matter how much we try to hide it from ourselves and others. We can see this, not by comparing ourselves to others but by comparing ourselves to God. We only admit to consciousness that which we have the courage to deal with. The pain of bringing those realizations to consciousness so that God can love them away is what spiritual growth is all about.

When we gather for prayer, as we stand together before God and each other at the Eucharist, we gather as sinners — one and all. There are no neat categories of good and bad, favored and unfavored. We are simply God's children — broken, sinful, lost, grasping, adulterous, and crooked in one degree or another. No one can see deeply enough to condemn anybody. We can see only externals. God can see into the heart. This God who sees all did not come to condemn but to save.

Our prayer, no matter where we sit in church, will not be heard until we recognize our own sinfulness, own it, and treat ourselves with the same compassion with which God treats us. When we are able to receive that compassion from God and from ourselves, we will be able to extend it to others. When we have done that, we will have finally learned to love God, our neighbors, and ourselves. When we will have done that, our Sunday Eucharist will have finally exemplified that parable of the wedding feast — a feast where the good and the bad are invited to sit down with the great King and bask in his love and compassion.

Scripture Readings

SIRACH 35:12–14, 16–18
2 TIMOTHY 4:6–8, 16–18
LUKE 18:9–14

Faithing

Thomas

*[These signs] have been recorded to help you believe...so
that through this faith you may have life.*

— JOHN 20:31

I PROBABLY haven't even given him a chance, but I'm not all
that crazy about Thomas the Apostle. It has to do with my
days at Saint Thomas Seminary. For six long years, four or
five times a day, I had to kneel in front of a huge old oil painting
of Saint Thomas sticking his hand into the side of Jesus. It was
like a huge billboard flashing, "Doubt! Doubt! Doubt!" What a
subliminal message for a teenage seminarian going through puberty in silence! We didn't need a six-foot Doubting Thomas
staring at us.

I want to talk about faith. I will try to be practical rather
than theoretical. That's not as easy as it sounds. I have this scary
quote from Matthew Fox in my journal: "If a teacher is not smart
enough, and in touch enough, to communicate his or her knowledge, then that person is in the wrong vocation." To talk about
faith to you in a convincing way, I have to be in touch with my
own faith. As you know, I speak more from my heart than from
books, so I don't write these things as much as give birth to them.
Here are some reflections on faith.

Doubt is healthy! Thomas was not some stubborn unbeliever;
he just had doubts. He wanted to believe, but he couldn't. Some
of us are like that. We try our best to believe, but we find it hard.
Most of us, however, have probably never taken the time to an-

swer two important questions about faith: (1) What do I believe? and (2) Why do I believe it? That would take a major spiritual search, and not many are willing to take religion that seriously. "Better let sleeping dogs lie!" Doubt, however, is not the same as that trendy social agnosticism that hasn't done its homework. Those doubters don't even know what they are rejecting. Healthy doubt, on the other hand, is an integral part of an act of faith. "Lord, I believe. Help my unbelief!" is not a bad place to be.

The opposite of doubting is "faithing." In English, the word *faith* is a noun — a thing — something to have or to lose. But in many languages the word is a verb, illustrating that faith is not something one can "own" but an activity that one "does." When we use *faith* as a noun, we might believe something or another is true, that it actually happened; but when we use *faith* as a verb, we believe it enough that the event or idea affects and underlies all our decisions, behaviors, and ways of relating. Then our faith is not in the truth of some event on the page of a book but has made its way into our minds, hearts, bloodstream, and cells. You know, we can have a lot of *beliefs* and very little *faith*. I am a believer, not just because I believe all this happened to Jesus, but because Jesus is alive and active in my life — because somewhere along the line, Jesus jumped off the page and into my heart. That's the difference between "having the faith" and "faithing."

For that leap to take place, we have to listen and study. Faith comes for most of us through hearing, not by sight. We are some of the millions of believers who are blessed with faith even though we have not seen. It is an awesome thought that, as a believer, you might be the bridge or obstacle for leaps of faith to be made. A welcoming heart makes it easier.

Faithing is a matter of entrusting oneself to the belief that we are guarded with God's power, and we can therefore trust rather than live our lives in fear. Faithing means that we operate our lives under the assumption that there is nothing to need, hide from, or fear. Faithing means that we operate our lives under the assumption that we are in good hands when in God's hands. Faithing can be frightening, because we have no assurance of the outcome. God may take us somewhere we would just as soon not go. God may give us what we desire, and we may find ourselves barely able to handle it. Faithing is simple but not easy.

The adventure of faithing is addictive. When you surrender to its power, you know that you have found "the pearl of great price" and that nothing else matters as much, even life's inevitable disasters. You end up identifying completely with Paul: "Our sole defence, our only weapon, is a life of integrity, whether we meet honour or dishonour, praise or blame.... [We are] always 'going through it' yet never 'going under.' We know sorrow, yet our joy is inextinguishable.... We are penniless, and yet we possess everything" (2 Corinthians 6:7–10 Phillips). Faithing is not just believing that the early disciples lived that way; it is about living that way ourselves.

We are guarded by God's power, so step out and start faithing! Take a few small steps, until you are able to walk with confidence. Know the difference between having the faith and faithing. It is like the difference between eating an ice cream sundae and looking at a picture of one.

Scripture Readings

ACTS OF THE APOSTLES 2:42–47
I PETER 1:3–9
JOHN 20:19–31

When the Going Gets Tough

Peter, James, and John

His face changed in appearance and his clothes became dazzlingly white.... [Moses and Elijah] were talking with him ... [about] his passage, which he was about to fulfill in Jerusalem.

— LUKE 9:29–31

I'M GETTING PRETTY TIRED OF IT! For the eleventh year in a row I am a "ten-million-dollar loser" in the American Family Sweepstakes. The very name Ed McMahon makes me sick. It's bad enough not to win, but I refuse to be called a ten-million-dollar loser. My last entry form, with my "valued customer, specially selected seven sets of personal numbers," had a warning in big letters: "James R. Knott could be the newest ten-million-dollar loser by failing to come forward before January 23." I came forward, but it looks like I'll have to live with the label "ten-million-dollar loser," at least for another year.

People who write sweepstakes promotional material are slick. With their computers, they can insert your name all over realistic-looking checks, insert your name in a list of potential winners, and almost make you believe you're already sunning on the beaches of Hawaii. The whole point is to get you to do such a good job of imagining yourself a winner that you will buy one of their magazines. They put the idea in your head. You imagine it. It works.

There is something useful about this dynamic. Just creating a useful image in a person's mind can keep that person going. Dreams and visions and mental pictures sustain people during hard times. These visions help prisoners maintain their sanity over long years. These dreams help refugees cross open seas in leaky boats in hopes of a new start in life. These mental pictures have sustained millions of soldiers far from home during dangerous wars. If we didn't have this ability to imagine, dream, and envision, we would not survive for very long. We would have no drive, ambition, or motivation.

Visions sustained most of the major characters of the Bible during hard times. Abraham and Sarah had one foot in the grave and were childless when God called them to father and mother a race of people "as numerous as the stars," and promised them a new homeland to go with it. That promise sustained them and kept them going during some very dark moments. Moses was called by God to lead his people out of slavery to a "land flowing with milk and honey." For forty years they wandered the desert, sustained by that dream and vision. Moses could see it and smell its breezes in his mind's eye, and he kept that vision alive in the mind of his people.

In Luke's gospel, Jesus was about to head out for his final trip to Jerusalem, where the cross awaited him. He retreated to a mountaintop for some guidance from his Father in heaven. Jesus would never take any step without the approval of God. He took his closest companions with him. Something tremendous happened there — something they never forgot. God gave them a sign that they were on the right path. God gave them a glimpse, a sneak preview, of glory to come. It was only a moment — it did not last long — but the memory of that experience carried them through days of suffering, death, and loss.

God's promises always come true, even those that seem totally impossible. But it can get quite tiresome waiting for them to materialize. God is a slowpoke, and he sometimes gets on our nerves. In times of darkness, loss, and setbacks, doubt and lack of faith can overwhelm us. We try to keep believing and hoping, but sometimes it is damned hard. Quite often we have nothing to go on but a promise. Sometimes we have nothing more than the memory of a previous time when God helped us.

But quite often God gives us one of those peak experiences that keep us going — like the one in Luke's gospel — those special, brief, and deeply moving experiences that keep us going through the dark times. It's like the familiar saying: "I believe in the sun even when it isn't shining. I believe in love even when no one is there. I believe in God even when he is silent." Peak experiences are God's way of telling us to "hang in there!"

Dr. Martin Luther King, Jr., the great gospel preacher and social liberator, received one of those "glimpses of glory" toward the end of his life. In his last speech, delivered the day before he died, King spoke these words: "We've got some difficult days ahead. But it doesn't matter now, because I've been to the mountaintop... and I've looked over. And I've seen the promised land. I may not get there with you. But I want you to know tonight that we as a people will get to the promised land. And I'm happy tonight. I'm not worried about anything. I'm not fearing any man. Mine eyes have seen the glory of the coming of the Lord."

Mine was a twelve-year-long path to becoming a priest. Holding on to that dream was very difficult. I felt very alone and unsupported most of those early years. What kept me going was the dream of being a priest some day. Looking back, I realize that I was given bits and pieces of hope as I went along — enough at least to keep me going.

Sometimes all we have to go on in living the Christian life are the promises of God. While we wait and trust, God often sends us those special moments and flashes, like the Transfiguration. At those special moments, we get a glimpse of the light at the end of the tunnel. Lent is a time to "go up the mountain" with our God — a time of prayer and special attention to God. It is during such moments of intense prayer that God bestows these special experiences. To have them, we have to spend some time with God. May you use the time of preparation well. May God open your eyes to those special moments of grace that will help you "keep going" and "keep the faith."

Scripture Readings

GENESIS 15:5–12, 17–18
PHILIPPIANS 3:17–4:1
LUKE 9:28–36

A New Leprosy

The Ten Lepers

As he was entering a village, ten lepers met [Jesus]. Keeping their distance, they raised their voices and said, "Jesus, Master, have pity on us!"

— LUKE 17:12–13

*L*EPROSY HAS BEEN AROUND for a very long time, but at the time of Jesus there was no disease regarded with more horror than leprosy. No other disease reduced human beings to such hideous wrecks for so many years. The fate of the leper was truly tragic on three fronts. Its victims had to bear (1) progressive and intense *physical* pain; (2) the *mental* anguish and loneliness of being completely and totally shunned by other human beings; and (3) the *spiritual* horror of a theology that convinced them that their disease was a punishment from God for some sin they had committed. Let's look at this triple whammy, one whammy at a time.

1. There were three kinds of leprosy. The first kind began with unexplainable tiredness, followed by discolored patches on the skin. Nodules started forming on these patches, especially in the folds of the cheek, nose, lips, and forehead. The face became so distorted that a person lost human appearance. Slowly the sufferer was reduced to a living mass of stinking, running growths. The average course of the disease was nine years, ending in insanity, coma, and death. Another kind of leprosy began with the deadening of the nerve endings, followed by ulceration, muscle waste, and tendon contraction that caused the hands to become

like claws. There was the gradual loss of feet, nose, and lips. This form lasted from twenty to thirty years. The third kind was the most common of all. It was a combination of the other two.

2. Besides the physical pain, a leper had to deal with the loneliness and isolation of being totally abandoned and shunned by family members, former friends, neighbors, and church. By law, the leper had to live apart from the rest of society, often finding shelter in caves and cemeteries. Lepers wore dirty rags, shaved their heads, covered their mouths, and had to warn others of their presence in the area by calling out, "Unclean! unclean!"

3. Finally, lepers, no matter how virtuously they had lived, were taught that their disease was a punishment from God for some sin they had committed. So the pathetic lepers not only had to suffer horrible physical and emotional pain but, worst of all, had to endure it and die with it, believing that God hated them as well.

Jesus encountered many lepers in the gospel, including the ten in Luke's gospel. Let's look at Jesus' response. Typically, Jesus disregarded the traditional categories of "clean" and "unclean," ritual taboos, and imposed quarantines. He not only allowed such outcasts and the forsaken to approach him, thereby breaking the religious law of his day, he made it a point to seek these people out. Because of this kind of disregard for religious custom, he was severely criticized by the Pharisees: "Look there! That man welcomes sinners and even eats with them!" These lepers broke the law by daring to speak to Jesus. Jesus broke the same law by speaking to them. Moved with pity, Jesus cured them. Even if Jesus had not been the instrument of a physical cure, he would have worked a miracle for them by speaking compassionately. It had probably been years since these poor human beings had felt that warmth and compassion, and it meant even more coming from a famous young man of God, the rabbi Jesus from Nazareth.

My friends, today we are facing a new "leprosy" — AIDS — and, unfortunately, not much has changed in nearly two thousand years. People among us — men, women, and children — are facing certain death after enduring painful and disfiguring symptoms. Many face isolation, shunning, and abandonment by families, friends, and churches. About half of all Americans who live with AIDS are homeless or are about to become so. At three of the six AIDS funerals in which I have been involved, the family was so embarrassed about their dead son, brother, or friend that they did not want anyone, sometimes including the priest himself, to know the cause of death. But the most tragic thing about many of these deaths is that the love of God for these people is called into question. One denomination "excommunicated" a dying member of its church for refusing to denounce his friends — the very friends who had given him a free home and offered solace during his illness. Religious fanatics can be the cruelest of the cruel. Ignorant bigots still crank out the worn-out theology that connects AIDS with a vengeful God — the very theology Jesus rejected nearly two thousand years ago. Religious bigots always make the same mistake: They assume God thinks the way they do.

Why do we treat this disease so differently from other diseases? Why do we keep this disease shrouded in layers of fears, phobias, and paranoia? The answer is, of course, that it is often associated with homosexuality. Even though almost half of the 1 million newly infected adults are women, it is still considered a "gay disease." Because we have not dealt with the reality of homosexuality, we keep trying to bury this disease under all that ignorance and paranoia, and we cannot seem to deal with this disease with the same sanity and compassion with which we deal with other terrible diseases. It's sad, but some people actually believe that if they don't like something enough, it will simply go away. Wake up, church, and smell the coffee! AIDS is upon us. It will soon be coming to a home near you.

My friends, we do not have a cure for the terrible disease of AIDS, but there are several things we can do. We must reduce the incredible ignorance that leads to so much cruelty. We must open our eyes to the myth of safe promiscuous sex and the reality of serious drug addiction. We must radiate the unconditional love of God and the heroic compassion of Jesus to everyone. We can surround those who are living with AIDS with all the love and support we can muster, especially those who have been rejected and abandoned. We can support caregivers — parents, siblings, buddies, friends, and volunteers. And we can pray. Prayer keeps us from giving in to the sadness, fear, and anger. Prayer helps us keep our hearts open when they want to slam shut.

This disease is making saints out of very ordinary people. I salute those who are managing to live with AIDS. Your courage in the face of pain, ignorance, and fear is truly amazing. I salute those who have died of this disease. May they forgive us for what we failed to do. I especially salute the caregivers. You, more than anybody, know that AIDS is not an academic issue or a list of statistics. It's the rawest kind of pain when it infects somebody you love. I salute the many others who have helped start homes and hospices for persons with AIDS, or who have helped keep the homes and hospices going, assisting people with AIDS to die with dignity and spiritual support. And I salute anyone who is working in our communities for the gospel values of peace, justice, fairness, and human life.

Scripture Readings

2 KINGS 5:14–17
2 TIMOTHY 2:8–13
LUKE 17:11–19

LOVE STORIES

From the Inside Out

This people pays me lip service but their heart is far from me.
— MARK 7:6

I HAVE A FRIEND who has a cat, a nice cat as far as cats go, but the damned thing has one very obnoxious habit: It likes to get close — suffocatingly close. If you're standing, it rubs against your leg. If you're walking across a room, it practically entwines itself around your feet. If you're stretched out on the floor watching TV, it tries to cuddle up to your neck, head, or shoulder. Given half a chance, it will actually sit across your chest or stomach! It is persistent. You can push it away time and time again, or you can kick it halfway across the room, and within seconds it comes back, trying to snuggle up to you even in 100-degree heat.

You may not believe it, but my image of God is more like that cat. I noticed it a long time ago, and so I have kept my eyes peeled and my ears tuned. The list is too long to enumerate, but look at some of the biblical images: God created us in his image and breathed his life into us. We are referred to as his family, his adopted children, lambs he hugs to his chest, his bride, and, in a motherly relationship, as chicks she gathers under her wings. In a powerful image, God tells Jeremiah to eat the scroll on which the Word is written. In the letter of James, God's Word is to be "internalized." In Mark's gospel, Jesus does not want robots observing rules; he wants a human response from the heart. It's not what's going on outside a person that counts; it's what's going on inside a person that's important.

God's ultimate embrace is the Incarnation: In the person of Jesus, God becomes a human being to express his love for us.

Jesus teaches his followers that the kingdom is within them. Even after that, when Jesus is about to die, what does he do but give us his flesh to eat and his blood to drink? Talk about "getting under your skin"! As he left, he promised to remain in the Spirit and dwell within us, calling us temples of the Holy Spirit. We are referred to as "earthen vessels" that hold a great "treasure" (2 Corinthians 4:7). We are the Body of Christ in the world, living through his presence and power, carrying on his work in the world.

God acts a whole lot like that crazy cat. If God can compare himself to a mother hen, it seems appropriate to compare him to a cat! It seems to me that he's all over us, smothering us with affection.

In the Scriptures, God seems to insist on an internal response from his people. The scribes and Pharisees equated religion and personal goodness with observing certain rituals and keeping certain rules. The religious legalist of Jesus' day might hate his or her fellow man and woman, take advantage of the poor, be full of envy, jealousy, concealed bitterness, and pride, but that did not matter as long as he or she correctly observed laws about cleanliness and uncleanliness. There is no greater trap for religious people than to equate religion with outward observance. Church-going, Bible reading, careful tithing, or timetabled prayer forms in themselves do not make a person holy. In fact, done meticulously, they can actually make a person unbearably proud and self-righteous.

The fundamental question is: Where is the person's heart toward God and the people around him or her? If a person's heart is filled with bitterness, grudges, pride, arrogance, and jealousy and lacks compassion, then all the external religious observances in the world are totally useless. God is not impressed by religious gymnastics and pious antics, but by a loving heart. This is not to say that rules do not have an important role to play. But fundamentally, God is not interested in slavery to a rule book; God's interest is in a heart-to-heart relationship. He wants to get inside our hearts, and he wants us to get inside his. Anything else is idolatry.

Idolatry is a constant temptation in religious circles — worshiping the object rather than its Creator; clinging to the forms of religion rather than its essence; making the essential accidental and the accidental the essential. When we do that, then we go through a period where we settle for external conformity rather than internal acceptance of the good news. We actually try through legal sanctions to make people holy whether they want to be or not. It is much easier, as Pharisees always know, to arrange for external conformity, because it is much easier to pretend to be religious than it is to actually be religious.

Many of us grew up in a religious system that was carefully and neatly arranged so that going through the motions could almost guarantee warm religious feelings. One's commitment might be rather weak, but the external supports propping up that commitment were quite powerful. Many of those external supports and props have collapsed, and we find many, many people floundering because they have discovered that, without the externals, there isn't much left. If our faith depends solely on the structures of an organized church, then it probably never was much to begin with. The collapse of many of the structures of external conformity since Vatican II has simply made our deficiency of faith painfully obvious.

This is precisely the challenge facing post–Vatican II Catholics. How do we keep going without an elaborate system of external supports propping up our faith? These days we have to be committed to something beyond the forms and structures, or else we will dissolve in anxiety and frustration. The great theologian Karl Rahner was probably right when he said, "The Christian of the future will either be a mystic or he [or she] will not exist at all."

Mysticism need not be a dirty word or something reserved for a few eccentric monks. Mystics acknowledge the enormity of the unknown, realizing that the more they understand, the greater the mystery is. They refuse to put God into little boxes and trivialize the mystery. Mystics love mystery, in dramatic contrast to those who need simple, clear-cut dogmatic structures. Jesus put it this way: "Unless your holiness surpasses that of the scribes and Pharisees you shall not enter the kingdom of God" (Matthew 5:20).

The collapse of our highly complicated system of legal, external observance is a painful dilemma for the church. Either the church will vanish like the dinosaurs, trying hopelessly to reconstruct old forms and worship them, or it can accept the challenge to move to a level higher than "legalisms" in our relationship with God. At the heart of this relationship is the hunger and thirst for holiness, actually falling in love with God, maybe for the first time. When that day comes, Jesus will not say about us what he said about the Pharisees in the gospel: "This people pays me lip service but their heart is far from me" (Mark 7:6).

Scripture Readings

DEUTERONOMY 4:1–2, 6–8
JAMES 1:17–18, 21–22, 27
MARK 7:1–8, 14–15, 21–23

The Prodigal

While he was still a long way off, his father caught sight of him and was deeply moved. He ran out to meet him, threw his arms around his neck, and kissed him.

— LUKE 15:20

*M*Y FRIEND ROGER died three weeks ago Thursday. He died alone in a hospital bed in another state. Even though he was only in his thirties, there wasn't a lot of sympathy for him. Roger was gay and he died of AIDS. He was afraid to die, because he was afraid of God. He thought because the people around him had rejected him, God was going to reject him as well. I tried to explain to him that sometimes even so-called religious people mistakenly think that God reacts to them the same way other people do.

I never met Roger in person. He lived too far away. His brother, who comes here once in a while, had asked if I could help Roger get ready to die. We communicated through letters and phone calls. I wish I could have been there when he died. It hurt me deeply that he died alone. I had talked to him only a few days before. Even his family was not there. They hadn't even told the local priest that he had AIDS. I guess it embarrassed them too much. They cremated his body and held a private service.

Before he died, I tried my best to explain to Roger the parable of the prodigal son. I really don't know if I succeeded. From his letters and calls it was obvious that Roger did not understand the parable. He died without really understanding that God loved him dearly, no matter who he was or what he had done. This parable tells us quite dramatically that God does *not* think the way we do. And we need to know that lest we, in the church, continue to do to others what we did to Roger: to confuse our fears and phobias with God's way of thinking.

Jesus did not write books, but he told parables, or stories, as a way to tell us what God is like. He was great at storytelling. The parable of the prodigal son is, I believe, his best. It should never have been called the parable of the prodigal son. The son is not the hero; the father is. It's not about the son's sin; it's about the father's love. It's a story about God's love for us. Jesus was put to death for this kind of story.

Many religious people in Jesus' day believed he taught too lenient a notion of God. Many religious people today still believe that. They can't accept the notion of God's unconditional love for *all* his children. They still like to judge who's good and who's bad, who's in and who's out, even when Jesus strictly forbade it. Many religious people still will not accept the teaching of this parable without a lot of "ifs, ands, or buts." They think it's too good to be true. They believe it's too dangerous to preach seriously. And so the Rogers of this world suffer for it.

Jesus had a habit of socializing with whores, religious dropouts, crooks, the diseased, and "losers" in general. "This man," the Pharisees and the scribes hissed, "welcomes sinners and eats with them" (Luke 15:2). So it was in response to their criticism that Jesus told this parable to them.

So, what's God like? Jesus says he's like the father in the parable. After having been insulted by his own child — a child who demands his inheritance before the father is even dead — the father gives in. After his son has lost that inheritance to craziness and gotten down with the pigs, the father takes him back. What's incredible is how the father takes him back. There was no punishment given, or conditions laid down. On the contrary, while he's gone the father watches the road and longs for him. "While he was still a long way off, his father caught sight of him and was deeply moved. He ran out to meet him, threw his arms around his neck, and kissed him" (Luke 15:20). The father commanded the servants to quickly bring out the best robe! Put a ring on his finger and sandals on his feet! We are going to have a feast! That, Jesus would say, is what God is like when we sin.

Abraham Lincoln was asked, shortly before the Civil War ended, how he would advise treating those in the South. He replied: "Let us all join in doing the acts necessary to restoring the proper practical relations between these states and the Union,...they never having been out of it." That, Jesus would say, is how God treats us.

It's almost too good to be true, isn't it? Well, for many in Jesus' day, it was heresy. They hated this story. They got so mad they plotted to kill Jesus. They believed in just punishment for sinners, not hugs, kisses, robes, rings, and parties. They were the older son in the story: They stayed home; they did all the right things; they kept the rules. Like a lot of "proper people," they wanted blood. They were jealous of God's love for sinners. But Jesus makes the point that God loves both sons — the one who stayed and the one who left. God loves all his sheep — the ninety-nine who stayed together and the one who strayed. God gives all his servants a full day's pay, no matter when they started to work.

Many "religious" people fear this story. They are scandalized by such teaching, even if Jesus did teach it. They fear it might seem to condone immorality. According to some, the story of the woman caught in adultery was left out of early versions of the gospels because they thought it might encourage people to sin. They had already begun to try to remake God into the stern judge they thought he ought to be. So-called religious people have always had trouble handling the God Jesus taught, because he loves too much to suit them.

Like the characters in this parable, Roger has a brother. His brother got married in the church, has lots of kids, has a respectable job, and even serves on the parish council. He is the model Catholic. Roger could not fit into all the socially approved categories, so he left home to live in the permissiveness of southern California. In trying to find himself, he contracted AIDS and died. But I am sure of one thing today: God loves them both. I am sorry that Roger could not believe that while he was alive, but I believe he does now.

What would you have told Roger if you were asked to prepare him for death? What would you do if you found out that your son or daughter is gay? What if your brother or uncle or cousin or friend were diagnosed with AIDS? How would you treat him? Would you be like the father in this parable? Or maybe like the older son? Jesus was scorned and finally crucified for this kind of compassion. I was threatened by a man with a knife in this church for preaching this message. Don't be surprised if the world hates you for modeling Jesus' compassion today. Compassion has a price.

Scripture Readings

JOSHUA 5:9, 10–12
2 CORINTHIANS 5:17–21
LUKE 15:1–3, 11–32

I'm Somebody!

You shall love the Lord your God.... You shall love your neighbor as yourself. There is no other commandment greater than these.

— MARK 12:30–31

"YOU ARE CREATED in the image and likeness of God." Do you have any idea what that means? Just think about it! You are created in the *image* and *likeness* of God himself. You are a temple of the Holy Spirit. You are a child of God! You've got some "God" in you.

God, I wish I had heard that when I was a child! It would have saved me a lot of inner turmoil and mental anguish. What I actually heard was quite different: "You can't do anything right." "You're never going to amount to anything." "Your ears are too big." "Your teeth are too big." "You're a skinny little runt." "You screw up everything you touch." "Don't try it; you'll fail!" "You ought to be ashamed of yourself!" "You're not worth a hill of beans!"

"You are created in the image and likeness of God." At middle age this is something I have just begun to understand. For most of my life I never heard this, felt this, or believed this. I can actually remember the first time I ever really heard an adult seriously raise the possibility that I might be "special" in any way. I did a fire prevention poster in the first grade. It won a regional contest. Sister Mary Ancilla thought it was really good and invited me to the convent on a Saturday to touch it up for the big contest. She coaxed me, encouraged me, believed in me, and treated me like a winner, even before I won. It wasn't winning a contest that was so important. I still remember how strange and different it felt to be proud of myself, rather than ashamed of myself, for a change. Even at six years old, it made a lasting impression.

The next time I was to have that feeling was at St. Meinrad Seminary, thirteen years later. The monks were wonderful. I arrived as a sophomore in college — insecure, bashful, underachieving, and with a bad case of low self-esteem. I remember one of the monks saying to me, "Ron, we are going to help you identify your gifts and talents and then do what we can to help you develop those. We won't measure you against someone else but against what your best is." I remember laughing to myself. "These people don't know me. They don't know yet that I don't have any talents and gifts. But it won't take them long to find out, I'm sure!" I thank God daily that those good people got hold of me when they did. They taught me to love and respect myself and to cut the mental chains I had inherited from childhood.

You are created in the image and likeness of God. In all my years as a priest, I have discovered over and over again that there are hundreds, thousands, even millions who have not heard it, felt it, or believed it — and therefore have not lived it. They are abandoned and neglected children. They are abused spouses. They are adult children of alcoholics. They are the poor and disadvantaged children everywhere. They are the millions of suffering people with low self-esteem. Some have acted out in destructive ways. Others just suffer from chronic unhappiness.

Love God, love neighbor, and love oneself. Jesus came to remind us of our true identity and to challenge us to reverence it in ourselves and each other. His good news to the poor, about which we hear so much, is the good news that *all* are considered worthy by God; all have rights; all have dignity. He insists that even though you may be oppressed, beaten down, diseased, or hated, no one can rob you of your divine and royal dignity. Underneath all the ugliness or problems that weigh so many human beings down, there is a child of God.

Jesus' mission and ours is to dig ourselves and each other out of the mounds of mental and physical rubble that keep us from seeing our true nature: images of God and children of God. Some of us are buried deeper in that rubble of self-hatred and disrespect than others. We are blind to our own nature and to the true nature of those around us: Each and every one of us is an image of God!

If I had a child, I would follow Pablo Casals's advice and say to him or her from the first day on: "You are a marvel. You are unique. In all the world there is no other child exactly like you.... You may become a Shakespeare, a Michelangelo, a Beethoven. You have the capacity for anything. Yes, you are a marvel. And when you grow up, can you then harm another who is, like you, a marvel?" That's how I would teach what this commandment means, rather than insist on its being memorized. I wish I had been taught this meaning earlier. That's what my life is all about these days: teaching love of God, love of neighbor, and, yes, love of self. That is why I have such a soft spot in my heart and in my preaching for those who do not love and appreciate themselves, those rejected by the world, and all those who are buried under the rubble of self-hatred and low self-esteem.

I have made a great discovery these last few years: I do have a vocation. All those painful childhood years were not a mistake; they were the schools in which I learned compassion. Having had the chance to find my way out, I am learning how to lead others out. I have finally learned to love my childhood and everybody in it. I am where I am today not in *spite* of that but *because* of all that. I could not do what I do today if I had not gone through all that. I do have a vocation, and the Lord was just preparing me for it all those years. I never thought I would reach the day when I could look back on all that pain and be thankful, but here I am.

Love God with all our hearts. Love our neighbors as ourselves. This is the essence of the Christian faith. In a nutshell, this is it. When asked which commandment was greatest, Jesus answered that these two are the greatest. The two have become *one* commandment. As Saint John points out, you cannot do one without the other. If you say you can, you deceive yourself.

Love God with your whole heart? For most of my childhood, I cannot say that I loved God. Respect, yes. Fear, definitely. Love, probably not. To love God with one's whole heart requires a freely given response. You can't make a person love anyone, even God. That's like forcing a child to "give Aunt Clara a big kiss." You can force the kiss, but you can't force the love. I fell in love with God when I learned about the God that Jesus spoke of. He taught us to call God not Sir, or Your Highness, or Your Honor, but Abba. Abba — the embracing, affectionate daddy who spoils his children rotten with kindness. The parable of the prodigal son was the key. The Father-God in that story said it all. That God was so homesick for his silly little boy that he waited and watched the road for him to come home. When he did, there was nothing for the son to fear — no lectures, no punishment beyond what the boy had done to himself: just hugging, tears of joy, and celebration. An Abba is what I had been looking for all my life. When I found him, I couldn't help loving him.

"Love your neighbor as yourself." Once a person has accepted that he or she is created in the image and likeness of God and that Abba loves all his children unconditionally, that person is ready to respect and love himself or herself and every other human being on the planet. The problem is that many people need to be dug out of the rubble of self-hatred and disrespect for others. In his ministry on earth, Jesus went about teaching people about Abba. No matter whom he met, no matter how much rubble of rejection and self-hatred they might be buried under, he dug them out. He took Mary Magdalene and loved her, saw in her that image of God that had been buried from her own sight as well as from the sight of others, and uncovered it. He did that for all those who had lost sight of it — poor, sick, rejected, and abused. By loving them unconditionally, he taught them to love themselves and others. He redeemed them.

My brothers and sisters, know that God loves you unconditionally. No matter what you have done or have failed to do, God loves you and accepts you. Yes, God wants you to love him back. But even if you don't, he still loves you 100 percent.

My brothers and sisters, love yourselves. No matter how beaten-down you may be, no matter how unworthily you have been treated, no matter how weak and insecure you feel, you are a child of God. You are created in the image and likeness of God.

You are a temple of the Holy Spirit. Nobody can take that away from you.

My brothers and sisters, every human being deserves your respect. They too are created in the image and likeness of God, even though that image may be buried deep from sight. That is why Jesus told us to love our neighbor — even our enemies. That vicious criminal, that abusive parent or spouse, that hurtful and hateful relative — all are children of God and part of the redemptive mystery. But it is buried under a lot of rubble. They're looking for love in all the wrong places. Try to see beyond the obvious. That is what it really means to love your neighbor, to see each other as God sees: into the heart.

Scripture Readings

DEUTERONOMY 6:2–6
HEBREWS 7:23–28
MARK 12:28–34

Let Go of It!

───── ✠ ─────

Unless the grain of wheat falls to the earth and dies, it remains just a grain of wheat. But if it dies, it produces much fruit.

— JOHN 12:24

*I*F YOU HAVEN'T SEEN THE MOVIE *Dances with Wolves*, you must. It's about the clash between the indigenous Native Americans and the white settlers on the American frontier — a racial, cultural, and religious clash. It certainly is not the typical movie about cowboys and Indians.

I was most fascinated by the clash between the settlers' and Native Americans' spiritualities. The settlers have always seen themselves as the *masters* of creation, while Native Americans have always seen themselves as the *servants* of creation. The settlers have always seen themselves as the *owners* of the earth, while Native Americans have always seen themselves as *guests* of the earth. The settlers *conquer* the earth; the Native Americans *reverence* the earth.

I had a flash of insight while I watched the movie. It dawned on me in that theater that one line from the first chapter of Genesis is behind the settlers' thinking and has led to some disastrous results: "Then God said: 'Let us make [human beings]....Let them have dominion over the fish,...the birds,...and all... animals.' God blessed them, saying: 'Be fertile and multiply; fill the earth and subdue it'" (Genesis 1:26–28). That is the antithesis of Native American spirituality. While they have striven to live in harmony with creation, those of European descent have a sad history of subduing it. That attitude still lurks behind such practices as clear-cutting forests, damming rivers, strip-mining

110

national forests, offshore drilling, toxic waste dumps, and unchecked pollution of every sort — all in the name of progress. Our greed and avarice have led to the slavery of those of African descent and the virtual extinction of Native Americans, along with their religion and culture.

One particular scene in that movie brought this difference home so vividly. The Native Americans depended on the sacred buffalo for food and clothes. They reverenced this beautiful animal, praying in thanks for each one they killed. In one scene the Native Americans came upon a prairie strewn with hundreds of dead buffalo, stripped of their hides by commercial hunters and left to rot in the sun. The Native Americans cried at the sight of the devastation, desecration, and the white settlers' sacrilege — a sin for which we have yet to beg forgiveness, a sin that we continue to commit in so many ways. And we had the gall to call them "savages"! Native Americans have had so much to teach us, but in our arrogance and greed we have been totally blind to it.

Native Americans sought to adapt to reality. The European settlers sought to adapt reality to themselves. That arrogant kind of thinking has left us spiritually handicapped. Instead of loving the truth, we have tried to make true what we love. The Native Americans' spirituality tells them to cooperate with creation, to use creation reverently, and to resist settlers' temptations to "own" or "conquer" it.

Buddhism teaches something very similar to Native American spirituality. Buddhism teaches about the "three poisons" of greed, hatred, and ignorance that corrupt us from within. It is these three poisons that underlie all human bondage and misery. This longing and craving to possess things can also be called addiction. Detachment, or letting go, is the way out of this misery. Awareness, embracing others, and generosity (the opposite of ignorance, hatred, and greed) become the spiritual practice of Buddhists, a practice very much like the spirituality of Native Americans.

But Jesus teaches us the same thing. He teaches us through the image of a grain of wheat that it is in letting go and detachment that happiness is created. For life to move forward, we must continually go through the process of letting go of our attachments, both mental and physical, and surrendering to reality, to the truth. It is the trying to hold on to things that creates so much human misery. It is letting go that brings human happiness. As with a grain of wheat, if you try to hold on to life, clutch it, and preserve it, the life principle is smothered. It is only when we let go, throw it on the ground and let it die, that it produces many grains of wheat. It is in giving — not holding on to — that you receive. Happy is the person who is poor in spirit, who does not try to grab and hold on to things, who is detached from things. Whether it is an old idea, an old relationship, or an old way of doing things, it is in *letting go* that we become free. It is by holding on that we are imprisoned. It is our attachment to things that we cannot have that causes so much human suffering.

Instead of dealing with the truth about life, we are constantly trying to rearrange the world and reality so that we can keep our attachments and addictions. We actually start believing we will die if we don't get what we want. Instead of wanting the truth, we try to rearrange truth to fit what we want. Instead of surrendering to reality, we try to remake reality through pretense, through choosing to go blind, deaf, and dumb so as not to have to deal with it. That's what Jesus means in the gospel when he says that whoever tries to hold on to his or her life as it is will lose it, while whoever lets go of his or her life as it is will actually keep it.

To stay alive, we must constantly let go of where we have been. Life is a matter of constantly letting go. It is when we try to hold on to it, preserve it, freeze it, that we actually lose it. We actually create a hell for ourselves when we refuse to deal with what is and continue to demand to hold on to what isn't.

Let me give you some examples. Consider the situation of a child from a dysfunctional home. That child can go through life angry and bitter because she did not have the parent she needed or wanted. Or she can let go of that idea about what her parent should have been and deal with what is. It is the mind's attachment to an ideal about parents that causes the pain. It is when the mind lets go of the need for her parents to be other than what they are that freedom is possible. Letting go of the idea and need for a perfect parent frees that child for living.

Or consider the situation of some parents who lose a child in a tragic accident. Some grieve and then go on with their lives. Others build a shrine to the dead child in his former room, resist the idea that he is gone, hold on to the dream of what should have been, and perpetuate their own suffering for years.

Or consider the church's ancient practice of male, celibate priesthood. The number of priestless parishes around the world continues to grow and grow. Instead of letting go of that form or way of doing things, does it not cling to what it loves rather than to the truth, perpetuating its own decline?

Yes, letting go is an integral part of life. It is when we try to hang on to, grab, hold, and clutch life that we actually kill life. I remember the scene in John Steinbeck's *Of Mice and Men* when Lennie hugs his furry little bunny so tightly to himself that he smothers it to death. Many of us do that in life. We create our own suffering by trying to hold on to too many things.

There is a story in the Old Testament that comes to mind. King David's child lay ill and dying. David fasted, wept, slept on the floor, and prayed. But after a week the child died. David went out of his room, took a bath, went to the temple, and came home to feast. He was able to let the child go when death became a reality. He did not try to hang on to the child after it had died. He went on with his life.

David understood what many of us do not: Reality has a way of going on whether we like it or not. We can hang on to what has been, or we can go with the flow. David was able to reconcile himself to reality, rather than attempt to get reality to adapt to his wishful thinking. In the garden of Gethsemane, Jesus does the same: "Father, if it is your will, take this cup from me; yet not my will but yours be done" (Luke 22:42). And on the cross Jesus demonstrates self-emptying once again: "Into your hands I commend my spirit" (Luke 23:46).

There is an important spiritual lesson here. Let the one who has ears to hear, hear it. Whoever tries to save his own life will lose it, while whoever loses her life will save it. Whoever tries to hold on to life will lose it, while whoever lets go of life will preserve it. Think about those areas of life where you experience mental suffering. You are creating the suffering by trying to hold on to something you can't have, instead of letting go and dealing with what is. Your freedom from that kind of suffering begins when you realize that you are creating your own suffering by refusing to let go and adapt to what is — be it a relationship that didn't work out, a child who did not turn out as you had hoped, a promise that wasn't kept, a favorite old way of doing things that has to go, or a terminal diagnosis. Holding on creates pain. Letting go brings peace.

Scripture Readings

JEREMIAH 31:31–34
HEBREWS 5:7–9
JOHN 12:20–33

Anointing the Sick

Jesus toured all of Galilee. He taught in their synagogues, proclaimed the good news of the kingdom, and cured the people of every disease and illness.

— MATTHEW 4:23

*T*HE SACRAMENT of the Anointing of the Sick began its demise in the twelfth century when it started being called Extreme Unction, or last rites. It began its comeback in 1974 when we began to call it again by its correct name, Anointing of the Sick. For the past eight hundred years, it was given almost exclusively to those whose death was imminent. The person receiving it was often unconscious. Today we celebrate this sacrament with those who are seriously ill — physically, emotionally, or spiritually.

There is no question about it: Jesus was a faith healer. The gospels are filled with stories of cures he brought about. There is no question either that Jesus gave his disciples a share in this power and told them to use it. The oldest written gospel, Mark's, records these words: "They expelled many demons, anointed the sick with oil, and worked many cures" (Mark 6:13). These original disciples passed it on to their followers. We read about it in the Epistle of James: "Is there anyone sick among you? He should ask for the presbyters of the church. They in turn are to pray over him, anointing him with oil in the Name (of the Lord). This prayer uttered in faith will reclaim the one who is ill, and the Lord will restore him to health" (James 5:14–15).

Down through the ages, people of every culture have believed, almost instinctively, that somewhere there resides a healing power that can be activated under certain conditions and that the alleviation of human suffering will follow. The power to evoke this healing is usually attributed to holy men and women, who evoke it directly from God through various ceremonies, such as the laying on of hands, anointings, prayers, or the touching of relics and images. Even modern science has admitted that these healers have often obtained dramatic results where medical skill has failed.

How does healing work? How do these healers effect their cures? In a nutshell, their cures are due to the belief of the sick person that releases the healing power already resident in the subconscious mind. The belief of the sick person, encouraged by the "healer," triggers an abnormal acceleration of a natural, God-given, healing power we all carry within us. The healer elicits belief from the sick person. That belief triggers healing power. Health is the result. This healing power was given to us when God created us. In that sense, God is the source of all healing.

In the New Testament, we read about Jesus the healer. He used touch, spit, water, and words, but he always insisted upon faith. "Because of your faith it shall be done to you," he told the sick (Matthew 9:29). Jesus evoked faith in the sick. That faith triggered healing. Health was the result. Jesus, the person cured, and the people all around gave God the praise. The power of healing was not in the oil or the words or even in Jesus, but in the sick person's ability to believe he or she could be healed. We see it bluntly put in the words of the gospel: "[Jesus] did not work many miracles there because of their lack of faith" (Matthew 13:58).

The process of all healing is a definite, positive mental attitude, an inner attitude or way of thinking, called faith. If you have this faith, you will get results. The problem is getting past the skeptical conscious mind and into the subconscious mind, where all healing takes place. The subconscious mind is very impressionable to the power of suggestion, but the conscious mind is constantly sabotaging the process with negative messages of "can't happen." Faith is an intense, positive, "can happen" suggestion to this impressionable part of our brain where all healing takes place. It is this part of the brain that knows what to do to repair or heal a cut without the conscious mind's even having to be aware of it.

If you have a physical ailment and you can muster the faith, the sacrament of anointing is for you. But you must *believe* that you can get better. Your faith and our prayers, the blessed oil, and the laying on of hands can bring about healing. If you are carrying around an old grudge that is making you sick and keeping you from enjoying life, anointing is for you. But you must *believe* that you can let go of that grudge completely. Your belief and our prayers, the blessed oil, and the laying on of hands can bring about healing. If you feel spiritually sick, without a personal, loving contact with God, anointing is for you. But you must want a new relationship and *believe* that you can have one. Your faith in having such a relationship, our prayers, the blessed oil, and the laying on of hands can bring about a melting of all the resistance you have carried to such a relationship.

Those of you who are skeptical of your own ability to believe should remember these words of Jesus: "If you had faith the size of a mustard seed, you would be able to say to this mountain, 'Move from here to there,' and it would move" (Matthew 17:20).

Scripture Readings

ISAIAH 8:23 — 9:3
1 CORINTHIANS 1:10–13, 17
MATTHEW 4:12–23

The Road Less Traveled

I am the vine, you are the branches. He who lives in me...
will produce abundantly.

— JOHN 15:5

DID YOU HEAR the old joke about the drunk who lost his car keys on a dark street one night? He was pacing back and forth under a street light, head down, desperately looking for his keys. Along came a man who stopped and asked what he was looking for. "I lost my keys down there," the drunk said, pointing into the darkness, "and I can't find them." The puzzled stranger ventured one more question: "Sir, if you lost them down there, then why are you looking up here?" Annoyed, the drunk looked up and said, "Because the light's better here, stupid!"

We humans are a lot like that. Ever since the Garden of Eden, we have been desperately searching for the secret to happiness, but most of us haven't been able to figure out where to find it. It's as if we're mice who keep going down the same old tunnels looking for cheese, even though there is no cheese at the end of the tunnels. As the old country song goes, we're "looking for love in all the wrong places." In a nutshell, we have been looking "out there" where it ain't, instead of "in here" where it is. Even though there is no cheese at the end of that tunnel, we're still not ready to give up the search.

This is precisely what Jesus' temptation in the desert is all about. Before Jesus begins his ministry, the devil tempts him with all the traditional dead-end tunnels for happiness. They are all variations of the same theme: Happiness is "out there" — in power over people, in material possessions, in being approved of.

Jesus rejected all of them, not because he was a spoilsport but because they don't work. Get it? And yet people are still madly in love with those tunnels, even though there really isn't any cheese at the end of them. Maybe next time.

Jesus did point to the right tunnel. He revealed that the tunnel that leads "inside" is the one with the cheese. He talked about an "inner kingdom" that can be accessed by changing one's *mind* rather than by changing *things*. Jesus taught that the world we live in is the way it is because people are the way they are. That's why Jesus didn't fix things but asked instead for a change of heart. Jesus knew that simply rearranging the externals is useless without changing those fundamental attitudes of people that produce the suffering the world experiences. We will have a new world, both as individuals and as a society, when we have a new mind. The answer is not in rearranging things outside ourselves, but in changing our minds and hearts.

Now the church is supposed to lead excursions into this invisible, inner kingdom that Jesus talked about. But it has often been run by people who have never experienced this kingdom themselves. Since the Emperor Constantine legalized the practice of Christianity, many Christians have been lured away from following the inner path to build yet another worldly kingdom, known to us as organized religion. Christianity as an inner path has not been lost. But it gasps for air in a top-heavy, monolithic institution that has become more and more obsessed with its own survival and with preserving its treasured forms than with leading excursions into the inner kingdom that Jesus preached.

The clearest signal that we are in trouble is the growing appetite the world is manifesting for spirituality, coupled with the fact that more and more people are looking outside organized religion for help. Recently at the Synod in Rome, the bishops discussed what to do with the growth of "New Age religions" and "cults." Of course, they repeated our traditional way of dealing with such things: They condemned them. I wanted to fly to Rome and yell, "People are going other places *because* they are not finding it here! Let's quit condemning and offer something better! We've got the answer, but it's buried under too many layers of stuff! We need more spiritual guides and not so many ecclesiastical executives!"

The church is *not* the kingdom; it points the way to the kingdom. We cannot credibly preach an invisible kingdom when all our energy goes into maintaining a visible one. We cannot credibly preach the mystery of death and resurrection when we are obsessed with holding on to the status quo and paranoid about change. We've got a lot of baggage to dump if we are going to be credible teachers of the inner path and not simply mechanics in a creaky religious institution. The world is begging for spiritual leadership. If we are going to compete with the artificial happiness industry, we are going to have to be a lot more convincing. We are going to have to find the pearl of great price and enter the narrow door. We are going to have to exude the joy of people who have found it, or others will increasingly look elsewhere and view us as a drowning old dinosaur.

People are looking for a religion that produces real change, real transformation. The church has that, but it is going to have to clean up its act if it is going to shine through in such a powerful, clear, and clean way that people will be able to recognize it. Instead we seem to be as tired and weary as the culture for which we are supposed to be light and salt.

This is a time of breakdown on all fronts, but this breakdown is a sure sign of breakthrough. In the history of religious traditions, renewal is often preceded by a perception that people have exhausted their search into the externals of life, and have lost access to higher forms within themselves. We are at that point in history again. We may be ready to look within again. The question is: Will the church be able to lead excursions into that kingdom within, or will it be too distracted by concerns for self-preservation? Like a woman in labor, the church is struggling to give life to something new, not sure of when it will deliver. But now that the process is underway, now that this labor has a momentum of its own, it stops only at risk to its own life. We must trust God now like we have never trusted before. I am filled with tremendous hope these days. We're shedding old skins in preparation for a truly renewed church based on inner solutions rather than on external solutions.

"I am the vine, you are the branches. He who lives in me... will produce abundantly." If your religion is not satisfying, not producing real change for the better, it's not because you haven't found the right parish, the right priest, the right program, or even the right denomination. Those are all outside you. The solution lies in going within. The solution is not in changing things, changing locations, or changing circumstances; it's in changing your mind, changing your heart, and changing your values. Distracted spiritual guides or imperfect church structures may be aggravating, but they provide no excuse, because they are not the real source of the problem. When enough of us convert the way we think, then everything we see around us will change — drastically. And if we don't, nothing will ever really change for the better.

That is precisely what Jesus wanted us to know. Cling to his vine and flourish. Cling to any other and wither. If we really know where the cheese is and understand how to get to it, there is no end to the progress we can make in genuine happiness. If we really know where the cheese is, we will quit wasting our time and resources being suckered by the escalating false promises of a very sophisticated artificial happiness industry that saps our energy and attention while leaving us increasingly stressed out and disappointed.

"I am the vine, you are the branches. He who lives in me... will produce abundantly." Now that we know where the payoff really is, let's try the other tunnel — the one that leads inside — the one that leads to genuine happiness, a happiness that cannot be lost or stolen or taken away by anyone or anything or any event.

Scripture Readings

ACTS OF THE APOSTLES 9:26–31
1 JOHN 3:18–24
JOHN 15:1–8

Prayer: Taking Life On and Taking God Seriously

Lord, teach us to pray.

— LUKE 11:1

*T*HERE'S ONLY ONE WAY to take a licking and keep on ticking: *prayer.* And I sure don't mean "saying prayers." "Praying" and "saying prayers" are as different as a tornado and a report of one. God and I have developed a very close relationship over the years. I spent my childhood with a "rage-aholic." I went through puberty in a seminary, in silence and under a cloud of guilt and fear. And now I am giving the best years of my life to a church that seems to grow more dysfunctional by the week. Because of this I am sometimes so overcome with sadness that I could cry. It's a wonder I have any sense at all. But I am in constant dialogue with the Abba (Father) that Jesus revealed. The only thing that has kept me from giving up or giving in to the sadness is this regular dialogue that I call prayer.

It took me a very long time to develop a comfortable prayer life — one that fits me, not just one out of the catalogue. I always felt "defective" about this in the seminary, where we were measured by how often we performed certain spiritual exercises. There was a basic quota. And there was, of course, a regular bevy of the nauseatingly pious bent on doing a little extra to make the rest of us look even worse. But many of those "prayer forms" just didn't appeal to me. To this day, I don't sit around reading a lot of prayers out of books. My prayer life is a lot more intense than that. My prayer life consists of arguing, screaming, praising, thanking, begging, crying out, and sometimes even ignoring God. I have even had some mystical experiences where I have felt God's presence very intensely. But I have also longed, like Jonah and Jeremiah, to throw in the towel on God. I often remember the words of the two women in the movie *The Color Purple:* "It ain't easy trying to do without God. Even when you know he ain't there, trying to do without him is a strain." But that's what a relationship is all about. It's the intensity and the tension that make it live.

I am not trying to emote about my spiritual successes and failures; the point I am trying to make is this: Prayer does not begin with methods, forms, or formulas. A passionate relationship with God evokes prayer from us. If we don't have that relationship, prayer forms, no matter how good they are, will leave us "rattling on like the pagans who believe they will be heard through the sheer multiplication of words." But if we do have a passionate relationship with God, then many of the traditional or contemporary forms will be useful in expressing our prayer.

I want to highlight three points about prayer that emerge from the gospel:

1. We can see what kind of God we go to in prayer.

2. We learn that we don't have to grovel or bribe good things out of that God.

3. We who cannot see the big picture must trust that God is separating what is really good from what merely looks good.

First, Jesus taught us to call God "Abba," a term for one of those hugging and squeezing daddies that are so rare except in children's dreams. You cannot have an energetic prayer life without a love-filled relationship with Abba. Nor can you have a love-filled relationship with a tyrant. You might do your duty, but you will not have your heart in it. It will be the chore of a slave. Second, he told us that we are free to jump into this God's arms, anytime, for an embrace of forgiveness or a favor. Third, if it's good for us, it's ours. We don't have to beg and beg, like the pushy neighbor in the parable. If it's good for us, then Abba wants it for us too. If it isn't, then it is withheld. We'll receive it when and if the time is right.

If you have that kind of relationship with God, all you have to do then is to practice trust in every situation that is hurled at you. Even if it looks bad, smells bad, and tastes bad, you can somehow say to that kind of God, "This must be good, so let me have it." If it is good, you can shout and dance your gratitude. Prayer is the love language between the one who gives life and a one who receives life. Prayer is that unspoken energy between a lover and the beloved. "Praying" and "saying prayers" are worlds apart. One is a volcano and the other a Fourth of July sparkler.

Prayer is about engagement with life and with our God. If you are relating to God and are engaged in the life he gives you, then prayer will roll out of you like water from a spring. Prayer is a trusting response to the mystery of God and the mystery of life, one event at a time. Prayer is a reconciliation with life, with what is — not a plea to escape it.

Prayer is about keeping your heart open when it wants to slam shut. Prayer is about fighting fire with love when you really want to fight with fire. Prayer is about hanging in when you feel like quitting. Prayer is about "taking a licking and keeping on ticking."

Scripture Readings

GENESIS 18:20–32
COLOSSIANS 2:12–14
LUKE 11:1–13

Shepherding:
Good and Good at It

I am the good shepherd; . . . for these sheep I will give my life.
— JOHN 10:11, 15

Louisville, Kentucky
November 30, 1979

Dear Father Knott:

You are hereby appointed Pastor of Holy Name of Mary Parish, Calvary, Kentucky, effective January 3, 1980.

Devotedly yours in Christ,
Thomas J. McDonough
Archbishop of Louisville

— — —

Louisville, Kentucky
May 6, 1983

Dear Ron:

It is with great pleasure that I write to confirm your appointment as Pastor of the Cathedral of the Assumption. The effective date for this new appointment is June 15, 1983.

Devotedly yours in Christ,
Thomas C. Kelly, O.P.
Archbishop of Louisville

— — —

The operative word in both of these old letters pulled from my files is *pastor*. *Pastor* is a Latin word related to *shepherd,* a herder of sheep. Thus, in the Latin translation of John's gospel, Jesus would be called *pastor bonus,* "good shepherd."

The church has chosen me to be "shepherd" of this part of Christ's flock. I have always been a little uncomfortable with the title of pastor. First, the role model you measure yourself against is the Good Shepherd himself, and no matter how hard you try, you can never even get close to measuring up. It's almost a setup for feeling defective — that feeling that you are never good enough or that you never do enough. On many a day you can feel more like the hireling than the Good Shepherd, even after you have done your best. Second, I have always been a little uncomfortable with the title of pastor because it is a time when the role is being redefined in an era of mistrust of authority and an atmosphere of anger and hostility, often directed at our all-male clergy. I feel powerless. Many of us are no longer sure how to be a pastor these days. Meanwhile the sheep are proliferating while the shepherds are dropping like flies.

I want to say a few words about three things: (1) Jesus, the Good Shepherd; (2) my vision of pastors in the church; and (3) those "pastors" in our midst called parents and teachers.

First, about Jesus, the Good Shepherd. As always, Jesus uses some ordinary situation or thing to teach people about God. It is hard for us to appreciate how important sheep and their tenders were to the people of old. It was from these animals that their very livelihood came. Sheep produced food as well as clothing for whole families. Sometimes children actually grew up with the sheep, going out with them all day as soon as they were old enough. No one would ever think of letting an irresponsible dimwit or coward take the sheep out. It would be communal suicide. If anything ever happened to even one sheep, the shepherd had to bring home some proof that the sheep had died — a piece of an ear or a bone or the fleece — *and* proof that it wasn't the shepherd's fault, or else there would be hell to pay. If the flock was attacked by robbers or wild animals, the shepherd was expected to fight to the finish, even to the point of death. A true shepherd never came home without his sheep. It is to this kind of shepherd *par excellence* that Jesus compares himself. Out of pure love and without any personal gain, the Good Shepherd did lay down his life for us. It was his will that not even one should be lost, but that all should be brought home to his Father.

Second, by extension, the flock is the church and the shepherds are its pastors. The church is undergoing a crisis now with its shepherds, both in quantity and in quality. I will not address the problem of numbers, but I will say a few things about the issue of quality. In the original Greek, the word for "good" in "good shepherd" is *kalos*. There is another Greek word for "good," *agathos,* as in "morally good." But the word here, *kalos,* means "a goodness that attracts." To me these words express the difference between a morally good manager and a leader in the church. We still have a lot of morally good pastors who cannot lead and motivate.

The good pastor in the church should be both *agathos,* a morally good manager, and *kalos,* a leader. Because of our present distrust of authority and our insistence that everything be democratic, we are tending to short-circuit the emergence of many good leaders in the church. Leadership is very different from a rotating committee chairperson. Leadership cannot be rotated. Not all good (*agathos*) people make good (*kalos*) leaders. Leadership is about articulating vision for the sake of continuity. Leadership has both a clear vision of direction and the ability to get others to embrace that vision as their own. Managers have the skills to implement the vision; leaders move people's hearts. Good pastors, in short, must be both *agathos,* good persons, and must also be *kalos,* good at being spiritual guides who can help put people in touch with God. Pastors must be more than good persons; they must be effective persons as well.

Third, parents and teachers of the young, you too must be *agathos,* good persons, but you must also be *kalos,* good in your role as parents or teachers. You must be not just a good shepherd; you must also be good at shepherding. Anything you focus on and give your heart to can be gradually improved. Good parenting is always a matter of laying down one's life for the sheep. Parents who are both *agathos* and *kalos,* "good" and "good at it," deserve our deepest admiration and support.

Jesus reminds us that love can be the only motivation for ministry or parenting or any other form of shepherding. If love is behind our efforts, then we need not fear that we are imperfect at what we do. Jesus once said to some judgmental religious leaders, when they turned up their noses at the woman who washed Jesus' feet with tears, dried them with her hair, and anointed them with perfume: "Little is forgiven the one whose love is small." I am sure that the Good Shepherd might say to us who are putting our hearts in our efforts that, in spite of our mistakes and failures, "much will be forgiven the one whose love is great." Let's keep praying that in our shepherding we will be both *agathos* and *kalos,* good and good at it.

Scripture Readings

ACTS OF THE APOSTLES 4:8–12
1 JOHN 3:1–2
JOHN 10:11–18

New Eyes, New World

*When [Jesus] saw the crowds he went up on the mountain-
side. . . . His disciples gathered around him, and he began to
teach them.*

— MATTHEW 5:1–2

I SAW a 3-D movie in an old theater in downtown Branden-
burg, Kentucky, sometime back in the 1950s. As we came
into the theater we were given a set of "glasses" made of
some kind of plastic filter or film mounted on cardboard frames.
They looked like disposable sunglasses. Without them, the screen
was an ugly blur of colors and shapes. You could tell a little about
what was going on, but it wasn't pleasant to watch. But put on
those special glasses and you were in for a movie like you had
never seen. It was in three dimensions. I remember one scene in
which the camera was following a truck loaded with lumber. All
of a sudden one of the logs fell off, and it appeared to be coming
right out of the screen, right into your face. I remember everyone in the theater screaming and ducking under their seats. This
went on during the whole movie — objects seeming to come off
the screen, and people screaming and ducking. The special glasses
made all the difference in the world.

I am convinced that many Christian people — maybe even
most Christian people — are looking at Christianity the wrong
way, like watching a 3-D movie without the special glasses. They
see something fuzzy. They see colors, shapes, and patterns, but
they don't see much that makes sense. It is not at all exciting. It's
boring. It's not something that attracts a lot of attention or excite-
ment. Because they are looking at it without the special glasses,

all they see is a blur of rules, regulations, obligations, restrictions, and duties. Without the glasses, religion is not something exciting and life-giving, but something that must be endured so that one will be rewarded in the afterlife. In the end, we put up with it and give it a token bit of energy because we are afraid not to. In the words of Jesus: "This people pays me lip service but their heart is far from me" (Mark 7:6).

What are these special glasses that we need in order to make sense of Jesus and Christianity? It is the concept of the kingdom of God. Unless we see things through that lens, we will not get a clear, sharp picture of what Christianity is all about. Our religion will be limited to an obsession with sexual or moral prohibitions, and we will get the idea that Christianity is merely a matter of avoiding sin so that we can go to heaven "up there somewhere," where you can have all the things you ever wanted on earth. It's a bit like "You kids be good and I'll take you to Disney World this summer." As sad as it seems, this is all Christianity means to thousands of people. No wonder religion is such a fuzzy, blurry bunch of nonsense to so many. It's like watching a 3-D movie without the glasses.

The phrase "the kingdom of God" is used more than one hundred times in the New Testament. Of those, it is used seventy times in the first three gospels. It is the kernel of Jesus' teaching. If we want to know what Jesus taught, what he meant, then we simply must know what the "kingdom of God" means. That is the set of glasses through which it will come into focus for us.

The first thing we need to know is that God has a plan. It's an old plan. It is what God planned from the beginning. He wants all of us to be happy, healthy, peaceful, and whole. When he finished making us in his image and placed us in the garden, he stood back and noticed how good it all was. But it wasn't too long before we came up with our so-called better idea. We were not satisfied with what God had done. We resisted. That resistance to God has been called sin. From Adam and Eve on, we have tampered with God's plan for our happiness by thinking we could do better by doing it our way. War, disease, poverty, hunger, and all kinds of problems have been the result of our efforts. The Old Testament traces the history of that rebellion against God's plan and the suffering we have brought upon ourselves by resisting God.

Even when we did these things to hurt ourselves, even when the bottom began to drop out of his plan, God promised that someday he would have his way. Someday we would all go "back to the garden," a return we have called heaven, the afterlife, the Parousia, and the kingdom to come. God will have his way in the end. Do we not pray for that in the Lord's Prayer? "Thy kingdom come. Thy will be done on earth, as it is in heaven."

That day began when Jesus began his ministry. He announced that the kingdom was at hand. God was ready to start the journey home to Eden, to start undoing the damage of sin, to start bringing us all to heaven. Jesus began by asking the people around him: Do you want to go to heaven? Do you want to start enjoying heaven right now? Do you want to get a taste of it now? Do you want to be happy right now? And then he told them: You can. Here is how you do it.

You have to repent. You have to change the way you think and the way you see things. You have to let go of your own plan and adopt mine. Your plan has brought you misery. Mine will bring you happiness. My plan for happiness, not just when you're dead but right now, is this. These are the changes you need to make to start enjoying that happiness right now.

Be poor in spirit. This does not mean that you will be happy if you are dirt-poor. It does mean that if you are one of those persons who think they will accomplish happiness by accumulating possessions and things in life, then change! Repent! Quit doing it! Start putting people first. Put your friends, family, spouse, and your relationships to them first. Then you will become truly happy.

Be sorrowful. This does not mean that you go around sad and depressed all the time. It does mean that if you are one of those people who are so cynical about life that nothing is right or wrong anymore and you just do your own thing, then change! Repent! Quit thinking that way! Start accepting responsibility for your own behavior and the effect it has on other people. Start seeing your sins as sins. You cannot accept God's merciful forgiveness if you do not even admit you need it. Once you admit that, then you will become truly happy.

Be lowly. This does not mean that you become a doormat for people to wipe their shoes on. It does mean that if you are one of those people who do not take care of, love, and respect themselves, then change! Repent! Quit dumping on yourself! Start looking at yourself as you really are — neither a doormat nor a big shot, but unique and precious in God's sight. Start respecting yourself, being truly good to yourself, and keeping God's sacred temple a fitting place for God to dwell and carry out his work through you. Then you will become truly happy.

Be hungry and thirsty for holiness. This does not mean that you become a saccharine, pious, religious bore. It does mean that if you are one of those persons who haven't learned a thing about God or made an inch of progress in the spiritual life since the days of the Baltimore Catechism, then change! Repent! Quit being religiously retarded! Grow up! It is hard as hell to try to feed spiritual food to a bunch of people who are not even hungry. In the church we have thousands of people trying to be adult Christians with an eighth-grade religious education. Start enrolling yourself in Jesus' school of discipleship. Then you will become truly happy.

Be merciful. This does not mean that you accept anything that people do. It does mean that if you are one of those people who are always judging others, always looking for faults, and rejoicing in their failures, then change! Repent! Quit dragging others down! Start encouraging the weak, comforting the hurt, lifting up the fallen, and welcoming those who are rejected and ignored. Then you will become truly happy.

Be pure in spirit. This does not mean that you keep your mind out of the gutter and free of sexual fantasies. It does mean that if you are one of those people who go to church because it is obligatory or who give to charity when they have leftovers, because they will get a tax break or public recognition, or because of guilt, then change! Repent! Quit it! Start giving to charity regularly and generously because you truly want to help another suffering human being, because you are thankful, or because you want to support a good cause. Be single-hearted. Start doing the right thing for the right reason. Then you will become truly happy.

Be a peacemaker. This does not mean approaching our dangerous world like a naive simpleton with shallow solutions, as if grinning and handshaking will solve it all. It does mean that if you are one of those persons who believe that billions more dollars spent on military arms will make us secure, then change! Repent! Quit going down that dead-end street! Our country has spent millions of dollars for nuclear weapons alone. It's not working. After all that expense, we are still not secure. In fact, we are farther away from security than ever. Start investigating other means. Start challenging world leaders on all sides to think of new ways to solve these problems. Find those new ways of peacemaking. Then you will become truly happy.

Don't be afraid of being persecuted for what is right. This does not mean being rigid and intolerant and religiously self-righteous. It does mean that if you are one of those people who are governed by what people like, what is popular, what others do, then change! Repent! Quit being blown about by the wind! Start taking a stand. Start living by principle rather than convenience, no matter how much it hurts or how much ridicule and rejection you get. Start living according to standards and principles. Then you will become truly happy.

These are Jesus' secrets to a happy life here and in the life to come. Start looking at your life and the people around you through these glasses, and then, maybe for the first time in your life, you will know what in the world Jesus was talking about. You will know what will make you really happy, now and in the long run. Live life looking through these glasses, and you will start living the kingdom now and start getting a little taste of what heaven will be like.

Scripture Readings

ZEPHANIAH 2:3, 3:12–13
1 CORINTHIANS 1:26–31
MATTHEW 5:1–12

Planting Seeds

This is how it is with the reign of God. A [person] scatters seed on the ground... [and] the seed sprouts and grows.... The soil produces... the ripe wheat.
— MARK 4:26–28

RECENTLY I WAS ON RETREAT with 160 of my brother priests from Louisville at St. Meinrad Archabbey in Indiana. While I was waiting for my ride to St. Meinrad, I found a packet of flower seeds that came free in the mail the previous winter. I poured them out onto a patch of dirt next to the garage. When I got back, I went out to look at the dirt. There they were, young flower sprouts, about an inch high. In a few months, they would grow into a patch of colorful flowers.

Jesus was very familiar with this process. He had witnessed it many, many times in his life. It reminded him of how God works in us.

Mark's gospel is not about farming tips but draws on the imagery of the sower: Thoughts and beliefs are sown in our subconscious mind. The subconscious mind is the "ground" in this parable. The "seeds" are the thoughts and beliefs we plant there. Positive thoughts and beliefs produce positive results; negative thoughts and beliefs produce negative results. Individuals, families, churches, or nations reflect what is planted in their minds.

Just as seeds need nourishment — heat, light, water, and fertilizer — to grow into mature plants, thoughts respond to another kind of nourishment — faith, persistence, confidence, and imagination. Just as no farmer would plant any old seeds but selects certain seeds depending on what he or she wants them to produce, we too need to be selective in what we allow to be planted in our minds. If we nurture good thoughts, we will see good results.

Three things, then, are necessary: planting, growth, and harvesting. First, a farmer must plant the seeds or there will be no harvest. In the same way, ideas must be planted and ideals imagined or there will be no results. Just as a farmer does not have to strain to make seeds sprout, once an idea is planted the power to bring the desired results rests with God. Second, just as a farmer accepts with confidence that the seeds will grow, we must accept that our thought-seeds will grow to maturity, without our worry, strain and anxiety. The third step is harvesting — accepting the results as they appear, even if they appear different from what we expected. To harvest our ideas, we may be called to do things such as revise our relationships, move to another city, or develop certain skills. Timing is important. There is always an orderly sequence in which events unfold.

There are two examples from my own life. When I was seven years old, Sister Mary Ancilla had us go around the room and tell each other what we wanted to be when we grew up. When my turn came I raised my hand and, from out of nowhere, said I wanted to be a priest. Where the idea came from is a mystery to me. No one had ever suggested it to me. I had no relatives who were priests. My parents never suggested it. The pastor and sisters never gave a talk about it. But by saying those words, I planted a powerful seed in my subconscious mind. When I was twelve, I told my pastor that I was ready to go to the seminary. The seed had already sprouted. That sprouting seed led to my leaving home at age thirteen to enter the seminary and to begin a long and arduous trip to ordination. At age twenty-six, the dream-seed that was planted back in the second grade came to fruition. I became that priest I had dreamed about most of my life. God handed me a seed. I planted it. God made it grow to maturity.

In 1983, Archbishop Thomas Kelly offered me an idea-seed: "I want you to come to the Cathedral of the Assumption and do something with it." I accepted that idea-seed and planted it in my mind and heart by saying "Yes." I imagined turning the place into a lively spiritual growth center, like a medieval cathedral. For about a dozen years, we at the cathedral have seen that idea sprout and grow and develop, slowly but surely, with God's help. It is now coming to maturity. The harvest is in sight. Like a farmer who looks at his growing wheat with amazement, I look at what that idea-seed has become and I am amazed. Just as a farmer relies on heat, light, water, and fertilizer, we have relied on the faith, confidence, persistence, and imagination of many good people.

The parable about seeds shows us that tiny seeds of divine power, once planted in our minds and surrounded with faith, determination, persistence, and confidence, can be brought to harvest. On reflection, many of you will see this pattern in your own lives. Maybe it developed unconsciously. Maybe it can be recognized only in retrospect. But what if you believed in this spiritual process, really believed in it enough to deliberately and consciously practice it? What if, instead of leaving the planting to chance, you were to deliberately plant dream-seeds, plant them with the confidence and faith of a farmer planting wheat? It would be the difference between riding in a car and driving a car, between leaving things to chance and doing things on purpose. Is this not what Jesus meant when he said, "Ask for something. Believe it is yours, and it will someday be yours"? I believe it is.

Are you open to the possibilities of this parable in your life? What thought-seeds do you plant in your own mind? Do you understand that this spiritual law — like produces like — has already operated in your life? You have already reaped what you have sown, be it good or bad. Why leave it to chance? Why not understand this spiritual law and begin using it to produce desired results? Why not be deliberate about what you plant? Why not believe that the results are as certain as the appointed time when wheat seeds, planted and nourished, will produce wheat? Whatever your dream, large or small, according to this parable it can come to pass. It is the way God works in us. I know for a fact that it works. I have experimented with it many times in the last several years, always with results. It works!

I wrote something a few years ago to help me stay focused

on seeing the Cathedral of the Assumption rise from the ashes. I believe it summarizes what this parable is trying to say. It is called "The Dream":

> Translating a dream into reality takes great courage. Doubt is a constant enemy. When doubt reigns, there is a strong temptation to let go of part of the dream as a way of resolving inevitable tensions. Success depends on the ability to remain enthusiastic, focused, and purposeful to the end.

Scripture Readings

EZEKIEL 17:22–24
2 CORINTHIANS 5:6–10
MARK 4:26–34

Bread for the Journey, Strength for the Trip

[Elijah] went a day's journey into the desert, until he came to a broom tree and sat beneath it. He prayed for death: "This is enough, O Lord!..." But then an angel touched him and ordered him to get up and eat. He looked and there at his head was a hearth cake and a jug of water.... "Get up and eat, else the journey will be too long for you!" He got up, ate and drank; then strengthened by that food, he walked forty days and forty nights.

— I KINGS 19:4–8

I KNOW IT SOUNDS PRESUMPTUOUS, but for quite some time I have felt like Moses leading a group of people across a desert to the Promised Land as I have led the Cathedral of the Assumption into its new identity. If we had known what we were getting into and how long it would take, would we have set out?

For about ten years I attended thousands of planning sessions, looked at hundreds of architectural drawings, attended scores of fund-raising functions, and delivered untold numbers of homilies. For the next year-and-a-half, all we had to keep us going through the dirt, dust, and cramped quarters were promises, pictures, and publications. We endured setbacks, grumblings, and raw nerves. But somehow we managed to urge each other on. We still held out for our dream to come true.

I have never been so focused on one thing so intensely for so long in all my life. I believed we were going to make it. When the time came, we were ready to see a big part of our dream come true: the completion of the inside of the main church. We could see it in the distance, at the horizon. Little by little, we got another glimpse of it. It actually came together right before our eyes. I simply could not wait for Thanksgiving Day, when we would march through the front doors and stand around the altar for the first time. It would not come a day too soon.

I find myself getting very tired these days and asking myself how I can keep going for the rest of the trip. After the church is finished inside, we still have at least two more years of work before we finish the whole project. When I get really tired, I find myself longing for the day when I can get out from under all this pressure, all these expectations, and all this concentration. Like Elijah, I find myself wanting to sit down under a broom tree and rest. And yet God keeps saying: "Get up and keep going!" I am determined to finish this project. With God's help, with each other's help and encouragement, we can and will finish this project together. God has given me several second winds over the years and will continue to give us bread for the journey. And no matter how tired I get, I realize that I am watching a little miracle take place in downtown Louisville. I am both proud and humbled to be part of it.

Elijah was tired and worn out. He wanted to quit. He was ready to die. He was a man exhausted from trying, a man who had worked his whole life for something, only to see it crumble before his eyes. All the miraculous deeds he did with God's help were about to evaporate. After standing up to the pagan culture that had been introduced to Israel, after his long campaign to bring Israel back to Yahweh, all his efforts came crashing down around him. This man was in despair. He had given in to hopelessness. Then all of a sudden, strength came in the form of bread and water, and he was able to keep walking, physically and spiritually, for forty days and forty nights. The help came from nowhere — "An angel touched him."

Elijah's story is for people who feel like they can't hang on much longer. This is a story for people who have suffered a deep and painful loss. This is a story for people who have suffered the complete shattering of their dreams. This is for people who have chronic pain and debilitating disease. This is for people at their wit's end. This is for people who don't know how they can keep doing what they're doing.

The mistake Elijah made was that he tried to rely on his own strength. It was not Elijah who brought people back to Yahweh; it was Yahweh who used Elijah to bring people back to himself. Elijah thought he had failed, even when it wasn't up to him.

Many of us make the mistake of failing to grasp the fact that God's strength is always available to us in our hour of need. Fear of starving is not the same as starving. Fear of running out of strength is different from actually running out of strength. The prisoners in Nazi concentration camps taught us that somehow, with God's help, we can keep going, keep hoping, keep praying, even when all hope seems to have evaporated. Many found a strength they never knew they had.

There is a growing number of people who come to noon Mass at the cathedral during the week. Numerous people, both men and women, have told me that they come to get their "fix." They work in stressful jobs, and that half hour of prayer rejuvenates them. We have not begun to tap the potential of the Sunday Eucharist. What if everyone of us started to realize that we can take enough fuel out of here to carry us through whatever happens next week? What if everyone of us started to see the Eucharist as *Viaticum*, "food for the journey"? But there is a huge difference between going to communion and communing, just as there is a difference between talking to someone and communicating with him or her. One's faith releases the power of this bread to bring strength. It is there, of course; but if it is to be effective, one must believe and commune.

The thing I love most about the church is that we serve "bread for the journey" to our people regularly. I can't imagine weekend services without it. It has strengthened throngs of people throughout the centuries to do things they thought they could never do and to endure things they never thought they could endure. If you have ever felt that Elijah's story is your story, then the Eucharist is for you. The secret is changing our minds — from "going to communion" to "communing with the risen Jesus." If your head ever gets in that space, you are plugged into the source of all power and strength. You, who thought you couldn't take another step, will find yourselves walking for forty days and forty nights, amazed at how you did it. It is not just about physical strength. Often, the hardest steps to take are the ones we take in our heads. Spiritual power is an even rarer commodity than physical power.

And so, "Get up and eat, else the journey will be too long for you!" You have a lot to handle. You have a lot of people depending on you. You have a lot to endure. "Get up and eat, else the journey will be too long for you!"

Scripture Readings

1 KINGS 19:4–8
EPHESIANS 4:30—5:2
JOHN 6:41–51

AN UNCONDITIONAL LOVE

Holy Thursday

But if I washed your feet —
I who am Teacher and Lord —
then you must wash each other's feet . . .
[for] as I have done, so you must do.

— JOHN 13:14–15

EVERY ONCE IN A WHILE some religious crusader gets the idea to carry a cross through some public place. I always chuckle to myself, because their crosses usually come equipped with a small set of wheels to make them easier to drag through the streets.

There is, of course, a world of difference between carrying a cross and reenacting a cross-carrying. When Jesus said, "Take up your cross and follow me," surely he meant a lot more than putting on mini–Passion plays on street corners. Hopefully, he meant a lot more than that self-inflicted gory masochism that is played out in some cultures' pietistic practices during the Lenten season. Surely he was speaking of embracing necessary and grace-filled pain — the kind of pain that transforms us, makes us grow in holiness, and enables us to develop our very best.

I suppose this is the pitfall of Holy Week in general. It can be reduced to the mere reenactment of our treasured, historic religious events. We "play" Palm Sunday, foot washing, and un-veiling the cross. All this symbolism is rich and good, but we cannot stop there. We must allow these events to affect us and penetrate our core. We must not merely reenact Jesus' deeds; we must translate them into our own language and times and find a way to live them. There are a lot of good and holy people carrying crosses these days who wouldn't be caught dead dragging a big wooden cross down the street, much less one with wheels. There are people who have dragged huge crosses down the street who have never "carried a cross" in their lives. It's not as much about reenactment as it is about translating these events into the events of our everyday living.

On Holy Thursday we reenact Jesus' foot washing at the Last Supper — that dramatic example of service from the gospel. But the real foot washing happens outside the cathedral. I have seen it outside my window overlooking Fifth Street.

I saw it when two of our hospitality ministers put one of our elderly widows into their car to take her out to dinner after Mass, before bringing her home to her small one-bedroom apartment. I saw it when another couple drove up to the curb in the pouring rain to unload one of our nursing home residents who depends on volunteers to bring her to her beloved cathedral from way out in the suburbs. I saw it again when our archbishop, after working a full day, dragged himself out again after supper several nights a week to confer the sacrament of Confirmation out in the rural parishes, or to attend a meeting somewhere around the diocese. I saw it early one Sunday morning in the scene of a single mother with three small, scrubbed children in tow, walking into the cathedral for children's choir practice. I can only imagine the extra sacrifice that woman went through to pull that off. I saw it on several days recently when I watched groups of office workers on their lunch breaks, huddled together under those old red canopies out front, handing out bologna sandwiches and cakes to our street friends. I have seen it time and again as generous and talented people go in and out of the Cathedral Heritage Foundation offices next door, giving of their time, talent, and resources to rebuild this old cathedral. Those are the things Jesus really meant by doing "foot washing" in his memory. It's about loving, unselfconscious service to others.

At the Eucharist we break bread and pour wine not merely as a reenactment of the Last Supper. This is not just another scene in an annual Passion play. We celebrate the *living* presence of Jesus in our community, just as our forefathers and foremothers have done before us and just as our children's children will do after we're dead and gone — until Jesus comes again. This eating and drinking makes us "companions" to one another. This eating and drinking motivates companions to do for each other what the Lord has done for us. This eating and drinking makes foot washing possible, makes foot washing understandable. We are able to do it. It makes sense to do it, because we are companions in the Lord.

Scripture Readings

EXODUS 12:1–8, 11–14
1 CORINTHIANS 11:23–26
JOHN 13:1–15

Some Kind of King

The people stood there watching, and the leaders kept jeering at him, ... [and] the soldiers also made fun of him, ... saying, "If you are the king of the Jews, save yourself."

— Luke 23:35–37

RECENTLY SIX JESUIT PRIESTS were dragged from their beds at their university on the edge of San Salvador and shot through the heads with high-powered rifles. Their cook and her fifteen-year-old daughter were also killed. The Jesuit provincial in Central America said: "They were assassinated with lavish barbarity. They were tortured before they died. They even took their brains." They were outspoken advocates for the poor and the abused. They wanted change, and that threatened the powers that be. Jesuits are known for their brains. In a most cynical twist, their murderers removed their brains from their skulls to make a joke.

In his first public sermon, Jesus had said that he too had come "to bring glad tidings to the poor, to proclaim liberty to captives, ... and release to prisoners" (Luke 4:18). This ministry and this message made Jesus immensely popular with the poor and outcasts of his world, and attracted the wrath and hatred of those in power. Jesus never wanted to be a king in the worldly sense of the word. He rejected that idea in the desert before he went public, and he shunned any talk of it when it came up. But those in power would not believe that he didn't want their power. They never trusted him. They were paranoid about it. So they had their day. They said: So you want to be a king, huh? We'll make you a king, ha-ha! Here's your crown! Here's your robe! Here's your throne! You wanted to save others, now save yourself, big-shot king! The leaders jeered, the soldiers made fun, and the people watched. They even tacked a sign over him that read: THIS IS THE KING OF THE JEWS! Ha-ha-ha!

Behold our king! That certainly doesn't look like any other king I know! Our king looks like a failure! Our king was abandoned even by his friends! Absent is the power, the prestige, and the pomp that we normally associate with the kings of this world! Our king is bathed in blood, sweat, and tears! We have a lot of explaining to do!

Those who had waved palms and shouted hosannas when Jesus rode so majestically into Jerusalem had no idea that things would turn out this way. They had their own plans for Jesus — plans for palaces, positions, and power — and this scene was not part of those plans. They knew Jesus could escape if he wished. He had saved others; why couldn't he save himself? They could not comprehend the fact that he willingly chose such a fate.

Why would Jesus willingly accept such a fate? He could have easily gotten around it; he could have escaped; he could have avoided all the pain. Either Jesus was the ultimate masochist or there is a point to all this. What is the point?

Jesus wanted us to learn something from his life and death. He wanted to teach us a fundamental lesson of life: You do not solve problems by running away from them or waiting them out. He taught us that problems are solved by confronting them, by facing them head-on. That which we cannot confront will control us. As the problems of life confronted him, he could have escaped them or avoided them and used his power to remove them. But he didn't. He chose rather to overcome the powers of evil and the problems of life — be they poverty, disease, rejection, hatred, corruption, even death — by taking them on and confronting them. He overcame and conquered them all by taking them on rather than avoiding them. He overcame his enemies by loving them. He overcame Satan by confronting him. He overcame all kinds of evil and sickness by facing them head-on. Finally, at the end of his life, he even overcame his own death by embracing it.

But most of all he wanted us to learn from all this. He wanted us to know this secret to happiness: that we can live that way too. He wanted us to know that we too do not solve problems by running away from them or waiting them out. He wanted us to know that we only solve problems by confronting them, by facing them head-on. He taught us that there is no way of solving the problems of life without first embracing them. When we avoid problems, we keep them. When we confront them, we shrink them and finally eliminate them. It's called the mystery of death and resurrection.

People in Alcoholics Anonymous know this. They teach us that the first step to recovery is facing the facts, by being able to say to the one in the mirror and then to others: "I am an alcoholic."

Avoidance is a short-term answer. Avoidance lets the problem grow and gain power. Avoidance settles for chronic, dull pain rather than brief, acute confrontation. The only way out of suffering is through it. Avoidance is tempting. Avoidance is our first line of defense. Avoidance is an art. When the present becomes too painful, we retreat nostalgically to the past; we drug ourselves against its pain or conveniently pass the blame and responsibility to others.

Whether it's a sin, a lump in your breast, a marriage that is decaying, a spending pattern that is destructive, an addiction to drugs, food, alcohol, or sex, or the imminence of our own death, we triumph over it by facing it, by embracing it. There is no new person without the death of the old. There is no cure without acknowledgment of the disease. There is no change without the pain of letting go. There is no resurrection of any kind without some kind of dying. That's what the cross means. That is what it means to say Christ is King.

We grow when we resist avoidance and choose confrontation. If we learn to do that as a way of life, we will someday be able to triumph over our own death by embracing it. Every day, life offers us some opportunities to participate in this mystery. And this King has promised us that if we are victorious over the small things, we shall be victorious even over our own deaths and reign with him forever.

Jesus challenges us to take on rather than avoid the problems and evils of this world. In the words of Dietrich Bonhoeffer: "Faint not nor fear, but go out in the storm and the action... [and] freedom will welcome your spirit with joy."

Scripture Readings

2 SAMUEL 5:1–3
COLOSSIANS 1:12–20
LUKE 23:35–43

Good Friday

Son though he was, he learned obedience from what he suffered.

— HEBREWS 5:8

T HE FIRST RECORDED WORDS of Jesus were spoken when he was twelve years old. Missing for three days, he answered his worried parents' questions by saying, "I must be about my Father's business" (Luke 2:49 KJV). Throughout his life Jesus struggled to do his Father's business: to do God's will, not his own.

At the very beginning of his public ministry, during his intense, forty-day-long desert experience, we see Jesus struggling with temptations to do his own thing rather than his Father's business. Before he works various miracles or when he is seeking direction in his ministry, we find Jesus in intense prayer, going back to the source, making sure he was doing his Father's business and not his own. In Gethsemane, the night before he died, we again find Jesus sweating blood over the struggle between his own will and the will of God. Because he had always chosen to do God's will in the small things, Jesus was able to choose to do God's will in the most critical moment of his life. Even as he died on the cross, Jesus deferred to the Father, giving his all with his last gasp of breath.

It was a struggle, every day in every way, for Jesus to let go of his own thing and do God's thing. Jesus was always able to say yes to God because he knew that if God wanted it, it had to be good, even when it did not look good.

As disciples of Jesus, we force ourselves to look upon the cross of Jesus — to take a long, loving look at that cross and all it implies. As disciples, we walk in his footsteps, take up our crosses, and follow him. We are not people who go out looking for pain, but we know that pain is a necessary part of the Christian life. As disciples, when we encounter these inevitable, necessary painful experiences, we, like Jesus, embrace them. Jesus taught us that "unless the grain of wheat falls to the ground and dies, it remains just a grain of wheat. But if it dies, it produces much fruit" (John 12:24).

Jesus taught us on Good Friday that the only way out of suffering is through it. By facing our dreads, we can shrink them and, finally, eliminate them. Confrontation of suffering is the only way out of suffering. When we see Jesus lifted up on the cross, we remember that even death was conquered by reaching out and taking it on.

Good Friday seems strange and almost absurdly out of place in our culture. People in our time tend to "freak out" when confronted with any painful reality. An awesome amount of energy goes into avoiding reality and keeping it out of our consciousness — energy expended on drugs, nostalgia, or materialistic distractions, to name just a few. Yet in many cultures, adolescents are sent through prescribed, painful experiences to prepare them for adulthood. When the young person is able to handle pain with endurance, he or she graduates into adulthood. These cultures invest years in preparing their young people to handle the pain of real life. In our culture, we spend those years protecting the young from any pain, teaching them to avoid it. Then we wonder why they are unable to function in adulthood. Ignoring the lesson of the cross, we produce generations of emotional, physical, and spiritual marshmallows. I suppose our culture's growing fascination with euthanasia and mercy killing is just another logical outcome of the illusory quest for a painless society.

The cross is part of our faith. Pain is part of life. Our world is riddled with pain, suffering, and brokenness. You see it in your city, sitting in your church, in your families, and on the news broadcasts from around the world. It doesn't have to be a starving Ethiopian baby or a weeping Nicaraguan mother; it can be that elderly woman dumped in any of dozens of local nursing homes, a child abused in secret in any of hundreds of private homes, a hollow-eyed street person, a cancer patient, an AIDS patient, a panic-stricken unemployed worker, or a spouse suffering through a boring marriage.

Whatever the pain you suffer, what the cross of Jesus teaches us is this: The beginning of resolution is acceptance. Deal with reality. By facing our dreads, we can shrink them and, finally, conquer them. In opening his arms to accept the cross, Jesus was able to conquer the cross. The only way around suffering is through it.

Scriptures tell us that Jesus "emptied himself." He let go of how he wanted things to be and learned to accept what God wanted — even death on a cross. Letting go is essential to discipleship. To move forward, we must let go of where we've been. Whether it is facing one's age, losing one's health or memory, or losing a person we love or a prized possession; whether it is yesterday's awards or today's glory, we have to move on. To let go, as Jesus let go, is essential to discipleship. Time and time again, from womb to tomb we have to let go. To let go is to die a little. It's painful — it can be bloody — but we must resist the temptation to cling to wishful thinking, to clutch at the way we want things to be, or to insist that things remain as they used to be. To give in to these temptations is to refuse to grow.

Death and resurrection is not a one-time event. Death and resurrection is a way of life. Jesus led the way. We must follow day by day, dying to our own needs and wishful thinking so that we can rise with Christ. As disciples, we can say "yes" to anything that comes our way. If God wants it, it has to be good, even when it does not look good. If we practice facing pain and letting go in the small ways, we will be able to say, with Jesus, in our last breath: "Into your hands we commend our spirits."

Scripture Readings

Isaiah 52:13 — 53:12
Hebrews 4:14–16; 5:7–9
John 18:18 — 19:42

Triumph of the Cross

If anyone who has been bitten looks at it, he will recover.
— NUMBERS 21:8

O N THEIR TRIP across the desert from the slavery of Egypt to the freedom of their new home, the people of God were beset by many woes. Just when they thought they were going to starve to death, manna for them to eat appeared from heaven on the desert floor. Just when they thought they were going to die of thirst, water flowed from the rock that Moses had struck so that they could drink. Just when it looked like the whole people would die from serpent bites, Moses created an image of those serpents and made the people look at it. Those who looked recovered.

Now this sounds like voodoo magic, but it isn't. It's primitive psychology. What Moses is saying to the people is this: Look at the very thing you most fear if you want to conquer it. It's looking away, not looking at what you fear, that will kill you.

Evasion is a good way to put off dealing with problems, but it doesn't resolve those problems. Postponing the pain merely perpetuates the suffering. The only way out of suffering is through it.

Moses' action — making an image of the thing that frightened people and challenging them to look at it — is still valid today. Looking the other way, refusing to deal with the painful realities in front of us, is killing us. Whether the painful reality is a growing cancer or the violence we read about every day, when we ignore what we don't want to see, we actually bring about what we most dread. Whether it's a tragedy like the massacre at Waco, Texas, or the violence in some private home, a solution begins with looking at it—looking at it until we get over it. It is *not* remembering and *not* looking that will make us sick.

We live in a world that has avoidance down to a fine art. If we don't like something, we look away. That's how violence has gained the upper hand. We have looked away too long because we just did not want to see. If we had seen, we would have had to do something. Lord Acton said it best: "All that is necessary for the triumph of evil is for enough good people to do nothing." We have looked away too much, and now we are suffering for it. Moses offers the cure: Look at painful reality and then you can deal with painful reality and, finally, conquer painful reality.

Scripture Readings

NUMBERS 21:4–9
PHILIPPIANS 2:6–11
JOHN 3:13–17

Easter Sunday

Remember, as yet they did not understand the Scripture that Jesus had to rise from the dead.

— JOHN 20:9

EVERYONE AROUND HIM seemed shocked that Jesus rose from the dead, even his very closest and dearest friends. No one ever loved Jesus as much as did Mary Magdalene, but she didn't station herself at the tomb waiting for the big event to happen. She was only doing what everybody else did after the funerals of their loved ones. It was customary to visit the tomb of loved ones for three days after the body had been laid to rest. It was believed that for three days the spirit of the dead person hovered around the tomb, but then it departed because the body had become unrecognizable through decay.

Jesus died on Friday. She was not allowed, by religious law, to travel on Saturday, the Sabbath. Mary Magdalene had to wait until Sunday to make her first visit. She couldn't wait. She got there before dawn. When she got there she was amazed and shocked: The tomb was empty! She concluded that the grave had been robbed. She ran back to town and got Peter and John. All three returned running. John got there first, followed by Peter. By the time Mary Magdalene got there again, Peter and John had left to tell the others. One by one, starting with John and ending with Thomas, they began to believe.

This is the Easter story. But what does it have to do with us? Was it done to evoke awe from the human race? To show us how powerful God is? Jesus did not seek to be worshiped; he sought to be imitated. If his life, death, and resurrection are to be imitated, then there must be some good in this death-and-resurrection mystery. In a society that teaches us that any and all pain should be avoided, the idea that some pain is good seems almost incredible.

The point of Easter is not simply that life is sometimes troubling and difficult but that, by its very design, it needs to be troubling and difficult. This is because it is not ease but affliction that enables us to develop our very best. The point of Easter is this: If we are to evolve into anything of spiritual quality and maturity, the only route is through pain and struggle. Those who grow the most are simply the ones who have weathered the most, endured the most, and struggled the most. And because such trial has been borne in the right spirit, they have been strengthened, enriched, and deepened the most by it. Think about any of the heroes or heroines of the faith, and one will always identify persons for whom hardship, sacrifice, and pain are no strangers. "No pain, no gain," as we put it today.

In short, we must not view death and resurrection as just an event from the past but as a life-producing way of living. No cross, no crown. No pain, no gain. People in recovery programs understand death and resurrection. People who have unilaterally forgiven their enemies understand death and resurrection. Parents who have had to let go of their children understand death and resurrection. Anyone who has ever embraced necessary pain and transcended it understands death and resurrection. It is not ease but affliction that enables us to develop our very best. The world does not understand this. It often teaches the avoidance of pain at all costs. This avoidance produces death, not life.

The best news of all is this: After embracing so many little deaths and transcending them, we will be able to finally embrace our big death and transcend it. "If we have died with Christ, we believe that we are also to live with him" (Romans 6:8). This is *not* all there is. We are not just celebrating Jesus' triumph over death; we are celebrating our own as well, no matter when and how it comes. What we celebrate is this: Death is not final.

Scripture Readings

ACTS OF THE APOSTLES 10:34, 37–43
COLOSSIANS 3:1–4
JOHN 20:1–9

Scared of
Your Own Shadow

*Jesus came and stood before them. "Peace be with you,"
he said.*

— JOHN 20:19

HAVE YOU EVER BEEN so overcome with fear that you could barely function? Maybe you were startled and your whole body convulsed out of control for a couple of seconds. Maybe it went on for a week or two as you waited for test results, your mind obsessed with that one thing to the exclusion of all else: "What if it's cancer?" "What if it's AIDS?" Can you imagine living in that state, day in and day out, year in and year out? Those of us who have lived with physical or emotional violence in our homes know how difficult it is to live in constant fear. Many of those who live in the inner cities of large urban areas know what it's like. Those who live in the war zones of Bosnia-Herzegovina know what it's like. Living in fear is a very heavy load to carry. To live in fear is to feel the presence of a ticking bomb, twenty-four hours a day, 365 days a year. It's no way to live.

In John's gospel, we see the disciples of Jesus cringing in an upper room, shivering in fear. The bottom had just dropped out of their world. They had just witnessed the gruesome execution of their beloved leader. They were terrified at the thought that they might be next. Peter had actually been identified in the courtyard the night of Jesus' trial. He lied his way out of being implicated. Every footstep outside the door sent them "up the wall." Every gust of wind drew a frightened gasp. They were terrified, panic-stricken, paralyzed.

Not only were they scared, but they were living with the fact that they didn't even have the guts to stand by their beloved Master in his darkest hour. Peter actually denied that he had ever heard of Jesus — not once, not twice, but three times. John, too young to be scared, was the only one of the Twelve to stay till the end. They were guilt-ridden, feeling worthless, demoralized, and very, very scared.

Then Jesus entered the room and said, "Peace be with you" — not once, but twice. Even though he had been abandoned, Jesus was back, loving them anyway. As with the forgiving father in Jesus' own story of the prodigal son, there was no scolding, no blame, no accusations — just "Peace": It's OK, It's all right, I'm here, Don't be afraid anymore, "Peace be with you."

They came to see that if Jesus could transcend all that he had been through, then no matter what happened to them, it would be OK. They knew that if Jesus could love them after what they had done to him, then nothing could be more certain than God's unconditional love. This knowledge that things are going to be OK, and that we are loved, produces an inner peace such as you would never believe. Peace does not exist "out there"; peace exists "in here." There is war "out there" because there is no peace "in here."

The opposite of peace, in the sense in which Jesus offers it, is fear. Fear does not attack us from the outside; we produce it from inside our own hearts. Fear is the product of negative thinking about possible disastrous results: fear of not being liked, fear of not being taken care of, fear of being abandoned, fear of being a failure. Fear is the result of not trusting God to be good to us. Fear is the result of having our illusion of control challenged. Peace, on the other hand, is the result of knowing and believing that we are loved, regardless; that everything will be OK somehow; that life can be trusted, implicitly. Peace does not mean that problems vanish. Peace simply means knowing and believing that problems are not the last word; that they should be put in perspective and we can even learn from them.

When I am writing or preparing a talk, I try to "feel" what the characters felt in the gospel. I try to recall a similar experience from my own life, even if it is only remotely the same. I ask myself: When have I ever experienced what is going on in this text? It helps the story come alive for me, and then I try to see if I can get my listeners to recall a similar experience in their lives. A successful talk, for example, helps people say, "Aha! I understand because I have been there too."

June 28, 1993, was such a day for me. It was the day the wall in the Cathedral of the Assumption cracked. This was not just another cracked building for me. It was as if the bottom dropped out of my world. It was as if every fear I have ever had came roaring out of every corner of my mind and heart and stared me right in the face: fear of failure, fear of being abandoned, fear of appearing foolish. Since then, I have experienced an incredible amount of peace. It was as if God said to me: "Excuse me, Mr. Knott, but this is my project, not yours!. I'm using you; you are not using me! Peace, Ronald!" The biggest challenge now is to work peacefully and wait patiently for God to bring this to completion. What is happening to me in the process is also important, just as the finished product is important.

Many have experienced the collapse of some familiar world: the death of a spouse, a divorce, an unfavorable diagnosis, the loss of a job, retirement, the loss of a child, a fire, or any of a host of other tragedies. Often these events leave people just as self-doubting, fear-filled, and anxious as were the disciples in the gospel story. But if you know the risen Lord, full of love and compassion, you will know that you are not in charge; that your life is being directed by a loving, compassionate Lord. You will know that you are loved. You will know that things will be OK, somehow. You will know that tragedies are not the absence of God but a certain sign that God is especially active, even in the most pain-filled times. You can enjoy peace even then, because you know that present problems are not the last word but instructive events that need to be embraced.

I believe this. I'm not just throwing out some kind of trite religious platitude. I grew up in a home filled with emotional abuse.

It was not good, but actually many good things have come out of it for me. My beloved mother died earlier than my emotionally distant father. It was not what I planned on, but one good thing came out of it: It produced the possibility of reconciliation with my dad. I was forced to go to the southern Kentucky missions after ordination. I did not want to go. Now I can easily see that it is part of the reason I ended up at the Cathedral of the Assumption. I have seen people in recovery grow into better people than they probably would have been otherwise. We even sing about this phenomenon on Holy Saturday. We call the first sin "a happy fault," since it took a sin to bring Jesus to us.

Never underestimate the positive effect tragedies can bring on — that was Jesus' message to his disciples. The message to you is this: If you are anchored to the risen Lord, you can have peace of mind and heart, right now, no matter how much pain, fear, or loss is going on in your life. Because under it all you know that you are loved and things will be OK. In the words of the traditional hymn "How Can I Keep from Singing?":

> No storm can shake my inmost calm
> while to that Rock I'm clinging.
> Since Love is Lord of heaven and earth,
> how can I keep from singing?

Scripture Readings

ACTS OF THE APOSTLES 4:32–35
1 JOHN 5:1–6
JOHN 20:19–31

Right under
Our Very Noses

*Jesus approached and began to walk along with them. How-
ever, they were restrained from recognizing him.*

— LUKE 24:15–16

I FIND IT DIFFICULT to live in the present. My mind is in the
future so much that I forget to savor the now. I have been
trying for years to break myself of the habit, with limited
success. I know there are a lot of marvelous things happening to
me, but I ignore them while my mind obsesses about tomorrow.
I am hopeful, because I used to be obsessed about the past. Now
that I have run off the road on both sides, maybe I will find my
balance in the center. I need to focus on today, where it's happening, not on a future that doesn't exist and a past that can never
exist again.

"Jesus approached and began to walk along with them. However, they were restrained from recognizing him." Luke's gospel
story has to be one of the most beautiful stories in the whole
Bible. It's about two people who were so focused on the past that
they could not see what was right under their very noses. Nobody
can tell a story like Luke. The bottom had fallen out of the two
people's world, and Luke paints a vivid picture of their hopelessness. They were walking to Emmaus, away from Jerusalem. They
were walking into a sunset. "Jesus approached and began to walk
along with them. However, they were restrained from recognizing
him." They halted in distress and said, "We were hoping" — past

tense — "that he was the one who would set Israel free" (Luke 24:21).

Here they were, walking and talking with Jesus and they didn't even know it. Their dreams about who Jesus was and what Jesus would do prevented them from seeing who Jesus really was and what he actually came to do. Their ideas about Jesus actually had blinded them to Jesus. He was with them, but their ideas restrained them from recognizing him. "We were hoping that he was the one who would set Israel free." When people begin to speak of hope in the past tense, they also begin to speak of God as though he were absent. What prevented these disciples from recognizing Jesus was that they were looking in the past rather than in the present.

All of us have walked the road to Emmaus — if not once, then many times. It is the path of fallen expectations, shattered dreams, and dashed hopes. Perhaps we have even found ourselves repeating the same haunting words: "We were hoping..." Perhaps it is a personal goal that we never realized, a marriage that didn't last, a child who "went bad," an unexpected illness, or a sudden death. One day we find ourselves walking with the same heaviness of heart that these two disciples experienced. Then we are faced with this question: Is God absent from us, or are we somehow absent from him as he continues to journey at our side?

Many of us experience God as absent from our lives. Many of us believe in God as a stranger from the past. Many of us have not allowed God to draw near enough to make a difference in our lives. The challenge thrown out to us is to recognize the God who walks with us and to speak with him as we walk along.

Assuming that God walks with us, unrecognized, the question remains: How do we recognize him? First of all, we must trust the present, no matter how it unfolds. Here, we must understand the difference between living in the spirit of expectancy and living with a set of expectations. Living in expectancy is to believe that a good God is running our lives and that every moment has the potential to be part of God's plan, no matter how hopeless it may appear on the surface. It simply means we live in unwavering trust in, and openness to, God. Expectations, on the other hand, are projections of our private wishes and needs. Expectations are our prefabricated plans that become the conditions we impose on the future. When we demand the future on our terms, we seek to limit God, and thus we set ourselves up for disappointment.

The two disciples had imposed a set of expectations on Jesus. "We were hoping that he was the one who would set Israel free." Jesus freed Israel, but in a much more radical way than their minds had imagined. Their plans for Jesus blinded them to the plans Jesus had for them.

My anxiety about the future is about confusing a set of expectations with expectancy. Something wonderful is happening at the Cathedral of the Assumption, but I want to control it rather than trust the One who is directing it. As one of the consultants on the renovation of the cathedral said to me: "This is bigger than any of us." My reply was: "This is bigger than all of us." Our job is not to be anxious, but to work as if everything depends on us and pray as if everything depends on God. That's the difference between living with expectancy and living with a set of expectations.

If you are facing a tragedy, real or imagined, you must do the same — whether it is a child who did not meet your expectations, a relationship that failed, or a goal that was never realized. Don't be so focused on your disappointment that you fail to recognize the presence of God in the reality that you had not planned. "Jesus approached and began to walk along with them. However, they were restrained from recognizing him." Sometimes things that turn out different from what we planned have in them the seeds of an outcome that is a million times better than we could ever have imagined. Often it is our attitude toward outcomes that turns them into tragedies. Just because things have not turned out as you expected does not mean that God is absent from you. It might mean that you are absent from him. It might mean that our expectations prevent us from recognizing the One who walks with us.

Scripture Readings

ACTS OF THE APOSTLES 2:14, 22–28
1 PETER 1:17–21
LUKE 24:13–35

Looking for God

He was lifted up before their eyes in a cloud which took him from their sight.

They were still gazing up into the heavens when two men dressed in white stood beside them.... "Why do you stand here looking up at the skies?"

— ACTS 1:9–11

As of this writing, I dedicated my life to the church thirty-seven years ago. I've spent twelve years as a seminarian and nearly twenty-five years as a priest. I've watched the stumbling of a once-arrogant church. Like an old movie star out of touch with her fading beauty, she seems to find herself embarrassed on a daily basis these days. But do you know something? I love her more now than I did thirty-seven years ago. Like an old alcoholic approaching recovery, she is going through that inevitable breakdown that leads to a breakthrough. It's messy, but it's real. I don't hate her because of her sins; I love her for her courage.

When I say "church," I don't just mean the Pope and the bishops; I mean us. We are the church. I believe we are going to get well. I see signs of hope and encouragement everywhere. I see and hear more people beginning to look for God all the time. I see and hear more and more people tiring of violence and the emptiness of rampant materialism. There are more people looking for spiritual growth than there are places that can deliver it. People are grazing across parish lines, denominational lines, and traditional lines, looking for something spiritually substantial. I see and hear people sick to death of second-rate preaching and obsession with religious organizational trivialities. I see and hear people looking for God in growing numbers.

"Why do you stand here looking up at the skies?" Where is God? For a few years, the early church stood around watching the heavens for Jesus to return. After all, he had promised to come back. They were content to sit and wait. The Feast of the Ascension communicates the realization of the early church: We are here to stay; we have work to do. No longer anticipating an imminent end of the world and Jesus' return in glory, the early Christians rolled up their sleeves to tackle the work. They transferred their gaze from the heavens to the world around them. It was in their everyday life that God was to be found — not in the past or future, but in the present.

Where is God? People are looking for God today in growing numbers, but the pickings are slim. Some look backward and romanticize the past. They believe that God was alive in the good old days, and if we could only return to the good old days, then we would find God again. They are playing vicious politics in every denomination from Southern Baptist to Roman Catholic. There are others who look for God in the extraordinary. Since they cannot find God in the ordinary, they run from one apparition and miracle to another. Cultlike groups are springing up around our church monthly these days. Secret messages, coded prophecies, and natural phenomena are their fuel. Others, weary of cleaning up this world, see God in the future. They yearn for the world's destruction by an angry God. They comb the apocalyptic clues for precise dating.

This Feast reminds us that God is right here, right now. And we must look around us, not behind us in a past that does not exist, or in front of us in some future that has not come about. God is! If we don't find God around us this day, we certainly won't find God in some museum or in some future yet to be.

Scripture Readings

ACTS OF THE APOSTLES 1:1–11
EPHESIANS 1:17–23
LUKE 24:46–53

Consecrated

I consecrate myself for their sakes now, that they may be consecrated in truth.

— JOHN 17:19

A CERTAIN WEASEL, long afflicted with neurotic symptoms, was accustomed to regular consultation with his psychiatrist, a wise old owl. As therapy progressed, the weasel, becoming disaffected with the long probing and the attempt to achieve insight into unconscious motivation and the wearisome effort to release emotional tensions, demanded of the owl, "Tell me what I should do!"

Taken aback by the unexpected nature and vehemence of the demand, the owl abandoned his customary reserve and ventured some direct advice. "I think, my dear weasel," he said at last, "that the only solution to your problem is to turn yourself into a frog."

The weasel was astonished at this advice and replied: "Thank you for your advice, which I fully intend to heed. One problem remains, however. I pray, sir, tell me how I go about turning myself into a frog."

To this the owl replied, with a certain measure of disdain: "My dear weasel, please be kind enough not to bother me with these operational problems."

God's unconditional love is a love that does not depend one iota on what we have done or failed to do; it is a love that pours freely out of God's heart to every human being. We are called — no, commanded — to love others, even our worst enemies, in the same way. So that I don't sound like the owl who gives theories but does not want to be "bothered by operational problems," I want to provide a few ideas about how to "go about" loving.

Contrary to popular opinion, love has nothing to do with feelings. To love, you must consciously make a decision to override your feelings for the good of others and then consecrate your life to that path. A consecrated person is one who is living intentionally, deliberately, and consciously. Consecration is what happens when you take loving seriously and put all your human and spiritual resources behind it! *Dedication* is too weak a word!

Jesus had that kind of relationship with our incredibly loving God. In order to reveal this incredibly loving God to human beings, he became love incarnate. In John's gospel, we find Jesus praying for his disciples. To us the disciples look like poor, bungling blunderers. After all, they had deserted him at his darkest hour. But here Jesus is, thanking God for them, calling them "gifts" from God. He is consecrated to them. He is about to leave them with a huge task, and he prays that they might catch his inspiration so that they cannot help but put their shoulders to the adventure, flinging themselves into living the love of God for all to see. Just as Jesus had consecrated his life to God, they would consecrate their lives to Jesus. Just as Jesus had laid down his life for his friends, so his friends would soon lay down their lives for Jesus. There is no greater love. Consecration is about making a stand and never wavering.

When I consecrated my life to God at my ordination, I did so as a human being making an unconditional commitment of love to God. What makes it so risky is the fact that I did it in 1970 — I was getting on the bus just when everybody else was getting off. I realize quite clearly that the priesthood is about as popular as the measles, but after nearly a quarter of a century, I have grown to love it even more. It has been lonesome much of the time. A few times, I have longed to get in my car, drive away, and never look back. But I'm still at it, not because I am lucky or because I can't do anything else or because the pay is incredible, but because I have prayed and worked hard to stay consecrated. I decided from the first day to nourish and cultivate and protect this commitment. I have prayed for courage, stamina, and passion, and I have received it. My prayer for the rest of the way is the same prayer that was said by the bishop during the ordination ceremony: "May the Lord bring to completion the good work he has begun in you."

What about you? Have you ever consecrated yourself to something or someone? The difference between a job and a vocation is the intensity of commitment. Is love some romantic, generalized, fluffy idea — a state of mind you fall in and out of — or is it a decision you have made and to which you are consecrated? Is your marriage something to which you have consecrated yourself enough to nourish, cultivate, and protect it with passion, through thick and thin? Or is it a promise you made, left to die on the vine, left to luck, left to starve from lack of attention? Many see marriage as an arrangement: If it works, it works; if it doesn't, it doesn't. Few really see it as a vocation to which they are truly consecrated.

The religious life, parenthood, and teaching the young are three more of the many other vocations that require that deepest kind of commitment called consecration. We are up to our necks with people in these professions and positions who are merely interested but not consecrated, and the results show it. They have "avocations," not true vocations. When I request an associate pastor, I want somebody who *wants* to be a priest, somebody who is *excited* about being a priest. Don't give me somebody who is going through some kind of identity crisis and doesn't know whether he wants in or out. Otherwise, he will end up doing more damage than good. The same can be said for marriages that drift into a coma two weeks after the honeymoon. The same is true for people who have kids without a commitment to parenting. The same is true for teachers who cannot or will not teach.

Like the owl, it is easy to claim love, talk about love, commit to love, but it is another thing to "go about" loving. Consecration is about a total commitment to "go about" loving. Needy people, looking to be loved, cannot consecrate themselves to love anything or anybody. They cannot love unless they have it to give. Consecration springs from the certain knowledge that we are lovable, at least to God, and that we are not as needy as we think.

Consecration is love under disciplined direction. First, consecration is deliberate love directed toward yourself. You must care about yourself and care for yourself. You must be consecrated to your own growth and care. Second, consecration is deliberate love directed toward God. A person who feels judged and hated by God has no possibility of loving God in return. Once that is realized, it is possible to be consecrated to God without always feeling defective and worthless. Third, consecration is deliberate love directed toward at least one other person — a spouse, a child, or a best friend. Only when one is capable of loving oneself can one expand that love to another, and then another, and then another, in ripples as far as the heart is wide. The greater the number of people we can embrace with deliberate love, the more we grow in holiness. Jesus was able to embrace us all. Our mission is to come as close as we can in imitation of him.

Scripture Readings

ACTS OF THE APOSTLES 1:15–17, 20–26
1 JOHN 4:11–16
JOHN 17:11–19

Get the Word Out: "We Are Loved!"

As the Father has sent me, so I send you.
— JOHN 20:21

IT CONSTANTLY AMAZES ME that people can go to church all their lives and end up knowing so little about God. The fact of the matter is, we have a God who is madly in love with us. He cares for us, and the funny thing is that he is so hooked on us that he can't help himself. The God who created everything is lovesick over the human race. That good news is so incredible that even the church, whose job it is to announce it to the world, has been so inept that we have the pathetic situation of churches crammed with people who wonder whether they are good enough or do enough to get God to love them. That God loves us, no matter what, is so incredible that we can't handle it. We keep putting conditions on it so that it will make sense and be logical, so that we can handle it.

The fact of the matter is that the God of all creation is madly in love with us and we can't handle that much love. Rather than accept it, we keep trying to explain it away with our ifs, ands, or buts. It's an incredible indictment of our churches that people can go to church their whole lives and still not know this. We keep talking about rules and regulations as a way of earning God's love. We are holy, not through effort but simply because God chooses to love us. We are holy because we are loved by God, not because we love. Some religious authorities still believe that we can scare people into loving God so that we can get God to love us back. It's as if God is up there blowing kisses, skywriting "I LOVE YOU" in big letters, sending candygrams, flowers, and singing telegrams; and we're sitting here in our little churches, gazing at our navels and wondering whether God is good, whether God cares, whether we can do enough to merit God's love, and whether God can forgive us for this or that moral failure. Yes, it amazes me how people can go to church their whole lives and end up knowing so little about God.

"As the Father has sent me, so I send you." God sent Jesus into the world to confirm what he has been saying all along. We were not getting the message. In spite of all the kisses, all the mysterious gifts, all the skywriting, and all the singing telegrams, we still didn't get it. So in time, God decided to come in person — in the person of Jesus, God in the flesh. Through word and deed, Jesus delivered the message that God is madly in love with us. He loves the sinner as well as the saint, the perfect son as well as the renegade, the obedient sheep as well as the disobedient one, the one who loves him back as well as the one who can't. Jesus delivered the message that God is so madly in love with us that we can even slap God on one cheek and he will turn the other, not once, but seventy times seven times. Jesus came to deliver the message that God is so madly in love with us that there is nothing we can do to get God to stop it. The only way we can try to stop it is to refuse to accept his love for us.

Once this sinks in, once we get it, once we walk through this narrow door, once we stumble onto this buried treasure, once we come upon this pearl of great price, our lives won't be the same. We will realize that we have been walking through a 3-D world without 3-D glasses. That's what conversion is all about: a new way of seeing things. That's why Jesus spent so much time with the blind, deaf, and dumb. He used one kind of blindness to talk about another.

So now that we understand that God's love is a given, that we don't have to go through some hoops and contortions to earn it, what does God want from us? He simply wants us to "get it," to know it, to understand it, to believe it, as incredible as it is: We are loved without condition! We don't have to be afraid. We can trust reality and live in confidence.

He wants us to get the word out. As God sent Jesus into the world with this message, so Jesus sends us into the world. Just as Jesus announced this good news from God in word and deed, we are called to get the word out in word and deed. We don't love ourselves and our neighbor in order to get God to love us, but because God loves us. It's a result of knowing we are loved and lovable, in spite of our sins. Underneath everything, there is basic goodness. That's our task: to comprehend our own worth in God's eyes, and to teach people about their own worth in God's eyes. We are asked only to love each other as God has loved us. We are asked to do that in word and deed so that others can also come to know it and feel it and live out of that knowledge. Ethical behavior is not a means to obtain love from God, but it's the result of knowing that you are loved. For the Jew and the Christian alike, there is only one sin: failing to love the God who loves you. God revealed not laws but himself.

Until we "get" this, we will never find our way out of racism, sexism, nationalism, starvation, war, and self-hatred. Until we "get" this, we will keep creating churches full of people who think religion is about rule making and rule keeping; we will keep creating a religion of holy days of obligation and Easter duties; we will see other people as competitors in a world of shortage; we will keep denying and projecting our shadows onto others so as to feel good and look good; we will keep creating churches that keep cranking out bad news, conditions, and condemnations because they simply cannot believe the good news itself.

The bottom line is this: We are loved right now, just as we are! The only question left is: What are we going to do about it? We have received an undeserved and unexpected invitation to heaven. The problem is not whether we have earned it or deserve it or are worthy of it, but simply whether we will say, "Yes, I will accept," or "No, I won't." All we are called to do is to say "Yes" and let others know through word and deed that they have the same invitation, and must also make the decision whether to accept or not.

So if we go to church because we think it is one way to get God to love us, we have missed the point. But if we go to church because we know that God already loves us, we have gotten the point. If we do good to others so that God will love us, we have missed the point. But if we do good to others because God loves us and them, we have gotten the point. People who have discovered this great secret — the good news — do not need rules and regulations. Appropriate behavior will come from the heart as a thankful response. The Eucharist, a weekly thanksgiving banquet, is so dull in most places, not because the priest is boring, the building is shabby, the music is pitiful, or the people are imperfect, but because we have buildings full of people who have only a vague idea about why they are there. For too many it's still one of those things they have to do to get something, rather than a response to what they already have — a freely given, unearned, and totally surprising unconditional love from the Maker of the Universe.

Scripture Readings

ACTS OF THE APOSTLES 2:1–11
1 CORINTHIANS 12:3–7, 12–13
JOHN 20:19–23

A NEVERENDING LOVE

Death

——— ✠ ———

Keep your eyes open, for you know not the day or the hour.
— MATTHEW 25:13

APPROXIMATELY two hundred thousand people died today. Some died by accident, some were murdered; some died of overeating, some of starvation; some died in the womb, some died of old age; some from thirst, some from drowning. Some resisted in fear and confusion; others surrendered with open minds and hearts at peace. But they all died, one way or another.

I had the flu last week and, even though there were points when I didn't care whether I died or not, I remembered Woody Allen's sentiments about death. He once remarked: "I don't mind dying. I just don't want to be there when it happens."

As the church year winds down, we are asked to consider death — our death. Human beings seem to have a problem integrating this reality into their consciousness. We seem to swing between morbid preoccupation with death and total denial of it. When I was a kid, religious artists seemed to me to be a bit preoccupied with the subject. Often, some studious saint would be pictured pondering the Scriptures, seated at a desk on which lay a human skull with the phrase *memento mori* (remember death) written on it. Modern-day Americans seem to lean more toward denial than preoccupation. We tend to share another of Woody Allen's sentiments: "I know everyone dies, but I was hoping an exception might be made in my case." Our tendency toward denial is supported by a funeral industry that promises to make dead people look "lifelike," and puts them in metal caskets that are "guaranteed for life." For just a few more dollars, you can get "perpetual care." Then, for some really big bucks, the industry offers the "deep freezer" option of cryonics.

I'm not about to give you one of those "If you don't shape up, you'll fry, bake, and burn" sermons on death. I want to "break open" the gospel and share its good news with you. After all, every time we get together around the altar table, we pray these words right after the Lord's Prayer: "We wait in joyful hope for the coming of our Savior, Jesus Christ."

In Matthew's gospel, Jesus uses the wedding feast as an image for judgment. The emphasis is not on punishment but on missing the party. I believe that we have been guilty for a long time of misreading these texts. Because of our crude, literal reading of the images, we have concocted conclusions that emphasize fear, dread, and punishment. I believe that Jesus really wants us to know that the tragedy here would be to miss out, through our own fault, on the wonderful things God wants to share with us. It's as if God has given each of us a winning lottery ticket and we have deliberately thrown it away. The tragedy is not that God punishes us but that we, through our own stupidity and carelessness, cut ourselves out. Hell, if it's anything, is the realization that we did ourselves in, that we refused to receive the unconditional love of God. God is so generous that to experience hell we have to really work at it. We should not fear what God will do to us but what we can do to ourselves.

We are called to live lives of readiness to meet God at any time; to live in "joyful hope for the coming of our Savior, Jesus Christ"; to live in the companionship of God himself; to live with an invisible means of support.

The parable of the ten virgins speaks of the tragedy of trying to get ready at the last minute. There are many who believe that the spiritual life is a bore and a chore to be put off as long as possible. Where did we get that idea? In the early days of Christianity, during the age of martyrs, holiness became closely associated with suffering. Christians were being tortured right and left. When that era ended, people were not sure how to be holy anymore. People began to take on ascetic practices. The pain that formerly had been inflicted by others began to be self-inflicted — severe fasts, flagellations, virginity, and celibacy. And general fascination with suffering became a synonym for holiness. Monasteries sprang up and institutionalized asceticism. The idea that clerics and nuns who inhabited these institutions were more holy than lay people has survived into our own time. Holiness became a matter of enduring life "in this vale of tears" rather than of enjoying one's life here in preparation for the life to come. No wonder people got into the habit of putting things off until the end.

The challenge facing the church today is to turn all this around — to change from seeing the spiritual life as a bore and a chore to be put off as long as possible, to seeing it as an adventure that produces happiness in this life. Jesus is quite clear that heaven has already begun and that we can start experiencing it on a limited basis right now. When I was a kid, I was religious because I was scared not to be — scared of missing out on the big prize in heaven. I pursue the spiritual life today because it produces its own rewards. You really can begin to experience heaven right here on earth. Expanding one's awareness is a lot more exciting than expanding one's bank account. An expanded awareness cannot be lost. There is no limit to its growth. Jesus was so right: "Blessed are" — present tense — "they who hunger and thirst for holiness; they shall have their fill" (Matthew 5:6).

We, as a church, must learn how to lead and direct people in spiritual growth. We must move beyond our recent thinking that holiness is a matter of conformity to rules and regulations, and teach people that it is an exciting quest with payoffs here in this life that continue into the next life. Death is tragic, not for those who have lived a spiritual life here but for those who live only in superstar Madonna's "material world" or, worse, for those who have never lived at all.

"Keep your eyes open, for you know not the day or the hour." If you live in the presence of God — if you have latched on to the kingdom in our midst, small as a mustard seed and quiet as yeast — it doesn't make any difference what day or hour anyway. Those who are ready will go into the incredible wedding feast for all eternity. "Eye has not seen, ear has not heard, nor has it so much as dawned on man what God has prepared for those who love him" (1 Corinthians 2:9).

Scripture Readings

WISDOM 6:12–16
1 THESSALONIANS 4:13–18
MATTHEW 25:1–13

For Better or Worse, I Will Be with You Always

And know that I am with you always, until the end of the world!

— MATTHEW 28:20

NOT TOO LONG after I was ordained, the oil barely dry on my hands, an angry young man verbally attacked me at a reception. He spotted my collar from across the room and made a beeline right to me. "Why in the hell are you wasting your time in that stupid church? I finally wised up and got out of that silliness a long time ago!" I was caught completely off guard. I stood there stunned and embarrassed. He proceeded to go through his (obviously well-rehearsed) litany of all that was wrong with church in general and mine in particular. He covered most of our sins: the Inquisitions, the Crusades, the bad popes, grade-school child abuse, the slavery of women, dull Masses, trivial sermons, money-grubbing TV preachers, and Vatican finances. I believe I was even blamed for Tammy Faye's hairdo.

That's an old story, but it has happened to me over and over again in my years as a priest, sometimes without the anger and sometimes with it. It seems that I have spent much of my time trying to give discouraged people reasons for hope. I believe that I have been preparing for this ministry from my early childhood. The fact that I came from one of those "dysfunctional families" that we all hear about *ad nauseam* makes it easy to survive in the dysfunctional family we call the church. I had to make the best of my family situation. I believe that God has been preparing me all my life to work in a messy, changing Catholic Church. I have learned the fine art of "making silk purses out of sows' ears."

I suppose the reason I have been attracted to the ministry of keeping hope alive is that I have not swept the problems under the rug. Rather, I empathize with many of the complaints I hear. The church has had, and does have, many problems. These problems are real, but there is something else going on too. I believe that this is the church, in sickness and in health, that Jesus founded. I believe that he is with us now and will be with us until the end of the world. The original Greek words, translated here as "always," literally mean "all the days." Jesus promised to be with us no matter what we may be like on any given day — when we're good and when we're bad; when we're heroic and when we're cowardly; when we're faithful and when we're not. I stay with the church and love the church, not because of human fidelity or infidelity, but because of the promise Jesus made in Matthew's gospel: "I am with you always, until the end of the world!"

My friends, faith is an option. You can choose to believe — or choose not to believe. If you choose to believe, you must look at the church's problems. But you must also look beyond them. If you choose not to believe, you can look at the church's problems and blame your choice on any of a million good reasons not to believe. Faith is an option. It's like the proverbial water glass: It's half full or half empty, depending upon the eye of the beholder.

When we celebrate the Feast of the Holy Trinity, we are not celebrating some cold, dry, theological concept; we are celebrating the reality of a living, loving God. God is not a thing. God is not far off. God is not aloof. The challenge of this Feast is to bring it out of dusty books and into our lives. We celebrate a God who is with us, "always."

Our God is a communion of persons: Creator, Redeemer, and Sanctifier. Traditionally, we have spoken of God as Father, Son, and Holy Spirit. In an age when we are examining the language we use to talk about God, I hope that we do not make God a thing in our efforts to remove sexist language from our theology and worship. Whatever we do, we cannot depersonalize God in our efforts to eliminate sexist language. I suppose we will not completely settle this problem soon or without a struggle. I won't argue here for either case. Wisdom and patience are prerequisites for resolving this important debate.

The doctrine of Trinity is an effort to speak of one God, revealed to us as a communion of persons. The essential thing is communion of persons. We humans are created in God's image. As male and female, together, we reflect that image. As interdependent beings, we reflect that image. As a church, a gathering of believers, we reflect that image. Just as God is a communion of persons, we are communal beings in God's image. Just as it is heresy to deny the Trinity, so it is heresy to deny our interdependence.

We became members of this faith community we call the church when we were baptized in the name of the Father, Son, and Holy Spirit. When we were baptized, we became "children of God." Those who believe that the church is "just an institution" from which they can "drop out" simply do not understand. Baptized in the name of the Father, Son, and Holy Spirit, that loving communion of persons we call God, we too are called to be church, a loving community of persons. If the church isn't that, then we are called to make it so, not to abandon it. Problems are simply no excuse to quit. God has promised to be with us always. We are called to live in common with God and others.

Scripture Readings

DEUTERONOMY 4:32–34, 39–40
ROMANS 8:14–17
MATTHEW 28:16–20

Second Coming

As to the exact day or hour, no one knows it, neither the angels in heaven nor even the Son, but only the Father.
— MARK 13:32

RECENTLY I DECIDED to go to bed early, thinking I would get a little extra rest. Wrong! The telephone rang about 11:30 P.M. The caller was a panic-stricken, rural-sounding man with a house full of kids screaming and yelling at each other in the background. He got my number out of the Yellow Pages. "Reverend, is the world going to come to an end tonight?" In my groggy state, I presumed for a minute it already had! Well, I have handled enough of these calls to know that a long discussion on biblical exegesis would not work. This man wanted a yes or no from an authority. So, without batting an eye, I answered with all the authority I could muster: "No, sir, the world will not end tonight. Please go to bed!" Well, he put his hand over the receiver and screamed to his brood: "He said it wouldn't end tonight!" There was a lot of muffled arguing before he came back on the phone. "The kids came home from school today saying some preacher had predicted the end of the world and all the kids were talking about it. They won't go to bed till you talk to them." Believe it or not, I had to talk to five kids, one by one, and tell them in the most confident voice I could muster: "Go to bed! The world will not end tonight!" The father came back on the line, thanked me, and hung up the receiver. I thought I'd never go back to sleep.

Jesus left this earth with a promise he would come back. Ever

since, his followers have periodically become obsessed with pre-
dicting the "end time." Nobody has been right yet. People at the
time of Mark's writing were obsessed with the belief that Jesus
was coming in their lifetime — any minute now! Mark's gospel
was the first to be written down. By the time Matthew wrote his,
the church was adjusting itself for a much longer wait. But even
Mark warns the people of his day — he tells those who were trying to predict the time — to go on living and leave the precise
time to God. Even Paul, after he had written to the Thessalonians
about the imminent coming of Christ, had to write to them a second time and tell them to get up and get on with life. They had
quit working and sat down to wait for the end.

Every time the world gets complicated and things appear to
be out of control, a significant number of religious people comb
the Scriptures and read the "signs of the times," coming up with
some dire predictions. Usually these people are fundamentalists
who read into both obscure Scripture texts and the signs of the
times and arrive at some bizarre and convenient conclusions. It is
almost as if they hope the world will end and then we won't have
to be responsible for the hard work of cleaning up the messes we
have made of it. Now, isn't that convenient? When it blows up,
we are relieved of all responsibility because "God predicted it"
and "God did it" — it's his fault. Poof! No more responsibility
for this "evil old world."

What about all those Bible-quoting doomsday preachers? Do
they know something we don't know? They seem to know the
Bible by heart. They say all the signs that the Bible talks about
are going on right now. Isn't it a signal that the world is coming
to an end?

Apocalyptic writing is very complicated for modern American minds. Typical examples of apocalyptic literature are the
Book of Daniel and the Book of Revelation, favorites among fa-
natic fundamentalists. It is not easily read but easily "read into."
Sometimes the more ignorant the reader, the more fascinated
and obsessed and confident in interpretation she or he becomes.
Since it is so obscure, symbolic, and allegorical, who is able to
contradict these self-appointed interpreters, except the most so-

phisticated biblical scholars? These fanatics are the people who hatch the hysterical situations like the one I have recounted.

What *is* the purpose of these writings? What are they trying to say? Well, the first rule in my book is this: If people use these readings to scare you, dismiss them. They were written in times of great stress to encourage people — the Book of Daniel to encourage Jews persecuted by the Greeks and the Book of Revelation to Christians persecuted by the Romans. They do stress that evil is powerful. We tend to seriously underestimate that power today. These readings stress that good and evil have some ferocious battles ahead, presented in a whole array of traditional cosmic symbolism. But the bottom line is this: Good will triumph over evil. As Saint Paul put it: "Eye has not seen, ear has not heard, nor has it so much as dawned on man what great things God has prepared for those who love him" (1 Corinthians 2:9).

The second rule in my book: Be prepared. The emphasis on preparedness and the return of Jesus is not so much on punishment and fear as it is on missing out on those great things. It is like having the lucky number in the Reader's Digest Sweepstakes and finding out you did not respond to the invitation to enter or realizing that you threw away your chances on purpose. We do not need to wait for the "return of the Lord" in fear, dread, and anxiety but "in joyful hope," as we pray at each Mass after the Lord's Prayer.

But we must always remember that the end will come, both for us as individuals and for us as a community. Mark uses the Greek words for "watch out." He warns us to watch out for those who would interpret events as a sign of the world's end. But even more, he warns the disciples to watch out for their own behavior. In other words, don't worry about the world ending; worry about living well, about being a good disciple. We need to hunger and thirst for holiness, to wait in joyful hope, and to keep our hand to the plow. If a person lives the life of a serious disciple, there is nothing to worry about and everything to hope for.

There is no better prayer for the end of the church year than the words the priest says at each Mass following the Lord's Prayer:

Deliver us, Lord, from every evil and grant us peace in our day. In your mercy, keep us free from sin and protect us from all anxiety as we wait in joyful hope for the coming of our Savior, Jesus Christ.

Scripture Readings

DANIEL 12:1–3
HEBREWS 10:11–14, 18
MARK 13:24–32